Black & White
and Pieced All Over

Stress-Free Foundation Quilts

Kay M. Capps Cross

Black & White
and Pieced All Over

Kay M. Capps Cross

CINCINNATI, OHIO
www.MyCraftivity.com
Connect. Create. Explore.

Other fine Krause Publications titles are available from your local bookstore, craft supply store, or online retailer; or visit our website at www.fwmedia.com.

13   12   11   10   09   5   4   3   2   1

DISTRIBUTED IN CANADA BY FRASER DIRECT
100 Armstrong Avenue
Georgetown, ON, Canada L7G 5S4
Tel: (905) 877-4411

DISTRIBUTED IN THE U.K. AND EUROPE BY DAVID & CHARLES
Brunel House, Forde Close, Newton Abbot, Devon, TQ12 4PU, England
Tel: (+44) 1626 323200, Fax: (+44) 1626 323319
E-mail: postmaster@davidandcharles.co.uk

DISTRIBUTED IN AUSTRALIA BY CAPRICORN LINK
P.O. Box 704, Windsor NSW, 2756 Australia
Tel: (02) 4577-3555

Library of Congress Cataloging in Publication Data
Cross, Kay M. Capps.
  Black & white & pieced all over / by Kay M. Capps Cross. -- 1st ed.
    p. cm.
  Black and white and pieced all over
  Includes bibliographical references and index.
  ISBN 978-0-89689-942-1 (alk. paper)
  1. Patchwork--Patterns. 2. Quilting--Patterns. 3. Black in art. 4. White in art. I. Title.
  TT835.C369 2009
  746.46'041--dc22
                    2008045125

Edited by Layne Vanover and Vanessa Lyman
Cover design by Nicole Armstrong
Designed by Julie Barnett
Production coordinated by Matt Wagner
Photography by Al Parrish, Tim Grondin and Adam Hand

Acknowledgments

I would like to thank:

F+W Media, Inc. for putting their trust in me.

Vanessa, my editor, for putting up with me!

Beach's Sew & Vac of Newport, Kentucky; Baby Lock; CM Designs, Inc.; Sulky of America; Specialty Product Sales, Inc.; Bali Fabrics, Inc.; Island Batik, Inc.; Marcus Brothers Textiles; Red Rooster Fabrics; Avlyn Fabrics; Maywood Studio; Robert Kaufman Fabrics and Windham Fabrics; all for providing amazing fabrics and supplies for me to play with.

My family for their continued patience, love and support—and also for putting up with the incessant "What do you think of this quilt?"

My friends for their love, encouragement and honesty.

My teachers for inspiring, shaping and leading me.

My students for showing up for class!

My Grandma Hap for binding to the end!

My dad for encouraging me to teach.

My He-Man for continuing to hold this chaotic life together.

My goddesses for providing so much joy.

Metric Conversion Chart

TO CONVERT	TO	MULTIPLY BY
Inches	Centimeters	2.54
Centimeters	Inches	0.4
Feet	Centimeters	30.5
Centimeters	Feet	0.03
Yards	Meters	0.9
Meters	Yards	1.1

Dedication

Hello, students! It's great to have you here! Do you realize how rich my life has become because of you? No, I didn't say how rich *I've* become because of you; my *life* is rich! We've survived language barriers, allergic reactions, machine malfunctions, supply snafus, nervousness and a host of other bumps, yet I walk away from each adventure supremely thankful that I had the opportunity to be with you. You question, cajole, tease, inspire and always delight me.

I can't thank you enough for sticking with me, traveling to see me, and helping me grow during this fabulous quilt quest. For you I want to be the very best teacher, designer, quilter and writer I can possibly be. With love and gratitude I dedicate this book to you—my students.

Table of Contents

Introduction

Paper piecing gives me hives. You may already know that about me (I don't keep it a secret). I'll elaborate for those of you that don't know; I abhor ripping out those pieces of paper, shortening my stitch length and having stress while stitching. However, the sharp angles and crisp lines that are possible with paper piecing are intriguing. My design sensibility is angular and asymmetrical, and those qualities are certainly possible to achieve with paper piecing. But is it the only way? Of course not! No-stress foundation piecing is simple and fun and yields terrific results. Any paper piecing pattern out there can be done with this method.

My first attempt at paper piecing was designing and stitching a large oval Mariner's Compass medallion. Talk about stress! The end result is in a box somewhere in my studio. I really should pull that out and finish it off. Remind me to do that when you see me.

Anyway, that adventure showed me that I love the look, but the method doesn't work for me. I played and experimented to find ways to create the look and provide accuracy while maintaining my loose working style. This book is a culmination of that practice and the teaching of these methods. Wouldn't it be great if we were in class right now and I could teach all of this to you firsthand? Since I am here and you are there, this book will lead you step by step through the methods. Using a wide variety of designs, you first will dip your toe in the quilting waters and then sharpen your skills with each successive quilt. I want you to enjoy foundation piecing as much as I do. It opens up incredible design and quilting opportunities that we shouldn't miss!

Speaking of opportunities, this is your chance to leave all of your ideas of how things "should" be done outside in the hall and jump in feet first! I'll be holding your hand the whole way. To get ready, let's go over a few ground rules. First of all, no stress allowed. Second, *mistake* is not a word we use. Third, *mistake* is not a word we use. "Oops" moments are merely creative opportunities, and opportunities are good things.

I'll give you all sorts of ideas for maneuvering through and making creative choices. Relax, and we'll take them as they come. Don't be surprised if you hear me shout out, "We have an opportunity!" I'll be grinning from ear to ear over your shoulder as you play and learn. We have an opportunity here together, so let's crack open the first project and get started. I'm right here beside you.

How Do I Get Started?

All black-and-white fabrics are *not* created equally. The bottom line is that a greatly reduced price equals reduced quality.

Chain and discount stores can purchase a well-known fabric design and print it on inferior fabric. That is confusing for consumers. We see the same design and automatically assume that it is the same fabric we saw in the higher-priced quilt shop. Not so.

When I invest time, effort and heart in a project, I want to use the very best tools. That translates to buying quality fabric from a reputable quilt shop. My grandpa taught me long ago that you get what you pay for. When it concerns quilting fabrics, he is absolutely correct.

Nothing beats a trip to the local quilt shop for selecting your fabrics. You cannot feel the texture of a fabric through a computer monitor. For me, fondling fabric is part of the joy of shopping. Quilting is a tactile experience, which starts with fabric selection. While I do my share of shopping online, I prefer being face to face with my choices.

One of the highlights of traveling and teaching is visiting the local quilt shops. I've never left without a package or two! Individual shops all have their own personality and feed my creativity in different ways. I don't want to miss a single one!

Sometimes I need a certain piece of fabric or some odd vintage piece. That is when I shop the Internet, which has a great many shops to choose from and peruse.

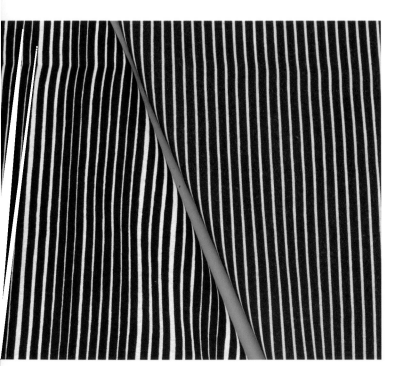

Selecting Quality Fabrics

Follow your instinct when feeling fabric. Very stiff and thin fabric will lose sizing and stability after it is washed. It will also lose color more quickly. This leaves you with cheaper, thinner, less vibrant fabric to create with. The fabric to the right is less expensive, but it is also less saturated, and the pattern, though similar, is less vivid.

Finding Vintage Fabrics

Shopping via the Internet is becoming more and more sophisticated and enjoyable. It will never replace the sounds, smells and atmosphere of a brick-and-mortar shop, but sometimes it supplies me with exactly what I need.

When you are building your stash, buy any fabric you absolutely can't live without. Even if that piece doesn't seem to fit with your existing fabrics, you can always pick up a few more pieces to go with it!

I look for scale differences and contrasting styles to complement and add to my supply. Variation is essential to an inspiring and user-friendly stash. Having a smattering of each scale in varying values is the key to a successful, well-rounded stash. Your stash doesn't have to be huge to be spectacular; it just needs to be diverse. That guarantees contrasting choices and vibrant combinations.

Buying Enough

I used to buy substantial yardage of any fabric I loved. Since there are more choices available, I don't have to do that anymore. I can be more selective and challenge myself to utilize a piece I love with less yardage.

Usually this works, but sometimes I regret not buying more when I come up just a little bit short on a quilt. Sometimes the fabric still exists, but the life of a print seems to be getting shorter and shorter. So, if you find a piece you know you will use in different projects, be sure to buy enough!

Choosing Plaids and Stripes

Don't neglect plaids and stripes when selecting fabrics. They are very useful and versatile building blocks for creating new quilts.

Using a Fabric Bin

It is so much easier to locate a certain fabric when it is sorted logically. That's why I use a fabric bin.

When an idea hits, I like to be able to go right to the fabric I'm thinking of and start creating. If I have to search for a certain piece, the idea may wither or lose momentum. I create in chaos, so the fabric bin is one area that is controlled and aids the process for me.

Testing Your Fabrics

Once you get your gorgeous fabrics home, prewash them and dry them. I like to make sure fabrics will hold up to washing and drying before I use them in a quilt I will give as a gift. If a fabric fades too much, I don't keep it. Fabrics that pass the test should be folded up and sorted by color and value.

Are All Foundation Piecing Patterns Created Equally?

I will use the term *foundation piecing* exclusively to represent both foundation-piecing patterns and paper-piecing patterns. I do not use paper for any of this type of piecing. Any paper-piecing pattern can be adapted to utilize my foundation-piecing methods, so I will refer to them all as foundation piecing.

With this type of piecing and the need to copy a design in order to create a quilt, the purchaser of this book is allowed to copy the foundation patterns for personal use. However, that doesn't imply that the purchaser can make twenty-five copies for neighbors, friends or guild members. Be respectful of copyright laws!

The difficulty of a pattern is determined by the number of pieces and sections in the pattern. The size of the individual pieces also affects the difficulty. Larger pieces are easier to put together, and smaller pieces require more care.

Foundation patterns will indicate how many different fabrics are required. Within that guideline, there are always individual choices you can make. If a design is scrappy, you can use fewer fabrics for a more controlled outcome. Or, you can make a design scrappy by substituting many fabrics of the same value for one fabric.

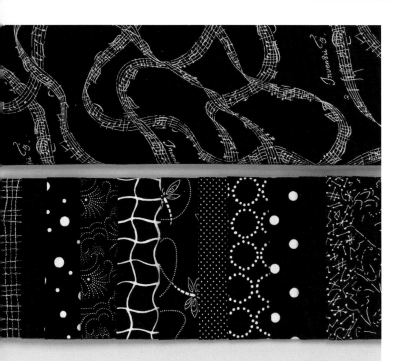

Making Adjustments
Substituting many fabrics of the same value for one fabric can give you that scrappy look.

Determining Difficulty
A one-section pattern (shown in top photo below) is typically less difficult than piecing together two or more sections (shown in bottom photo below) to create a block.

Most foundation patterns are already reversed for your piecing use. There is an easy way to check. If the design on the pattern is a mirror image of the quilt picture, then it is already reversed. If designs on the pattern and the picture are facing the same direction, the pattern needs to be reversed. To do this, simply trace it with a dark pen on plain white paper. Then flip the paper over and trace the lines to the other side of the paper, and the pattern is reversed!

Some patterns need to be enlarged before use. If you are instructed to enlarge a pattern (for example, see the Royaltry "preparation" instructions on page 66), the easiest way to accomplish that is to find a copy business that has enlarging capabilities. Some personal copiers and printers also have this option.

Enlarging can also be done the old-fashioned way: the basic grid method. Grid the original pattern in 1" increments. Grid a large sheet of paper with the enlarged increment (e.g., 2" for a 200 percent enlargement), and draw the design square by square. Unless this sounds fun to you, I wouldn't recommend it. I consider myself far too lazy and a "nondrawer," so this option isn't one I use. Lead me to a machine that enlarges, so I can get on to the fun part of quilting!

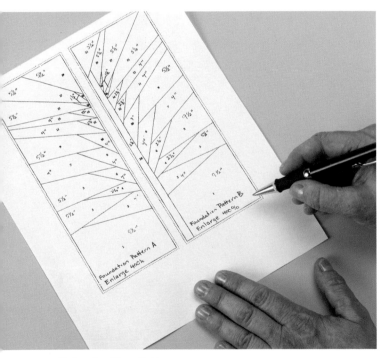

Enlarging Your Pattern

If you have a pattern that needs to be enlarged, like this example, the easiest way to accomplish that is to find a copy business that will do it for you. Your own personal copier or printer may be able to perform this function, but you might need to enlarge sections of the pattern at a time and then tape them together to make the whole pattern. As a last resort, you can always use the basic grid method to draw your own enlarged pattern.

Checking Your Pattern for Piecing Use

If the design on your pattern is a mirror image of the quilt picture, then it is already reversed and ready for your piecing use.

What Do I Need to Foundation Piece?

The tools for foundation piecing are basic but crucial for improving the fun and no-stress elements of this method.

The most important tool is a basic sewing machine in good working order. Nothing adds stress like a cranky machine. For optimum success, use a new needle on each project, and clean out the dust bunnies in the bobbin casing.

You will also need several basic sewing tools: rotary cutter, cutting mat, scissors, your favorite quilting ruler, pencil, pen and white paper.

A few specialized tools are also essential. An Add-A-Quarter™ ruler is strongly recommended for making this method fun and easy. For tracing multiple copies of the same design, the Sulky Iron-On Transfer Pen is indispensable.

A wooden iron or similar tool and a small cutting mat are also handy to keep next to your sewing machine.

In addition, I recommend two foundation fabrics: Tacony No-Show Mesh stabilizer and Sulky Soft 'n Sheer™ stabilizer. These are nonwoven nylon foundations that can be left in quilts. One of the things about paper piecing that makes me itch is tearing out all of that paper when the sewing is done. You don't need to tear anything out when you use these foundation fabrics, and the thin foundation doesn't add measurable weight or stiffness to quilts.

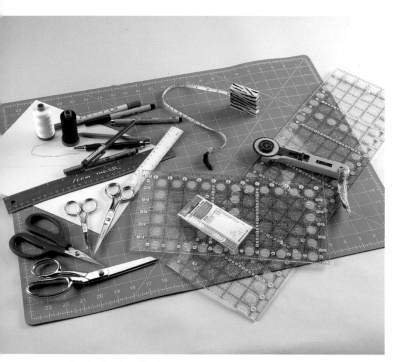

Basic Sewing Tools

Specialized Sewing Tools

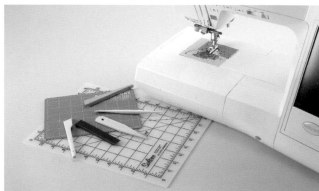

Irons and Cutting Mats

If I am doing a foundation quilt that isn't precision or based on a set pattern, I also use muslin. It adds weight, but sometimes I leave out the batting in favor of a muslin foundation. It provides an old-fashioned heavy yet flat feel. One disadvantage of using muslin is that you can't see through it easily. That keeps me from using muslin with a traced foundation design.

Aside from my preference for the two foundations I mentioned on page 16, I make no strict brand recommendations. Your tools can be whatever brand you are comfortable with and enjoy using. I do encourage you to stick with one brand of ruler to do the critical measuring (e.g., squaring up the blocks), since measurements do vary from brand to brand.

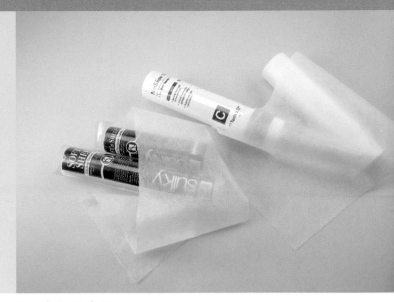

Feet for Foundation Piecing

If you are working with a ¼" foot that has a flap (left), switch to a regular foot (right) when working with the foundation fabric on top. While the flap is great for guiding you (no brain cells involved!), it can catch and snag the foundation.

Foundation Fabrics

I have used about every foundation out there and have settled on Sulky Soft 'n Sheer™ stabilizer and Tacony No-Show Mesh stabilizer for their strength and see-through-ability. Because they are nonwoven nylon foundations, they don't need to be removed from quilts.

Using a Leave-In Foundation

With paper piecing, all paper is removed after stitching is done. That requires you to shorten your stitch length to perforate the paper more, and more stitches equals more time sewing. Forget that!

Using a foundation that gets left in the quilt allows you to maintain a normal stitch length. There will be no pulling and tugging at the stitches for foundation removal, so you can also skip backstitching at the beginning and end of each line. Another time-saver!

If you really like to spend time picking out little tiny pieces of paper from a block that took extra time to sew (since the stitches were shorter), have at it. I choose the lazier, easier way for quicker, less stressful stitching.

What Fabric Should I Use?

My fabric selection method goes something like this: grab and go, then think and rearrange.

I initially like to select more fabrics than I need for a project and audition them. If there is one piece I absolutely want to use, I work around that fabric.

I then shift the pieces around and look at all of the possibilities with the fabrics I've pulled. Gradually the stack gets whittled down to the number of fabrics I need.

Next, I look at value changes, scale differences and depth of contrast to develop the desired palette for each quilt. I keep playing until the stack resonates: When the combination is just right, it just sings.

1 Select the focus fabric.

2 Whittle down the possibilities.

3 Develop the palette.

4 Finalize the fabric choices.

How Do I Trace the Design?

There are several ways to trace a foundation-pieced design. The easiest way is with a light box. While a lightbox makes the job easier, it certainly isn't essential.

I use the window in my studio door. You can take a design with foundation fabric layered on top, hold it up to a window, then use natural light to help you see the tracing line. To hold your layers in place, simply tape the layers to the window.

If the pattern line is dark enough, you can put a plain white sheet of paper under the pattern and then lay the foundation fabric over the pattern, without the window. The white paper helps the contrast show through, and this may be enough for you to see the line and trace it.

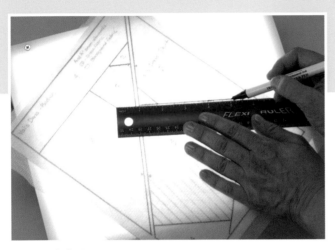

Using a Light Box

Tracing With Natural Light

Using a Sheet of Paper

Use Caution When Tracing

With this method of foundation piecing, you do not trace all of the lines and numbers. The foundation fabric will be left in the quilt, and traced numbers could show through the finished quilt. Do not trace any of the numbers or fabric codes onto the foundation fabric. You will use the original pattern for reference when it is time to sew.

19

In traditional paper-piecing, the block design is transferred to paper by tracing or copying on a copy machine. If you need 20 blocks, that means 20 tracings. I'm not that patient. So I stream-lined the process to duplicate the block design. You'll need regular copy paper, a Sulky Iron-On Transfer Pen, your choice of fabric foundation, a regular ruler or straightedge, and the printed pattern. We will trace the pattern once and wind up with many copies from one tracing. How cool is that!

1 When you're ready to begin, lay the foundation fabric over the pattern. Start by tracing reference points for the block. Mark each corner on the stitching line, but do not trace the entire stitching line.

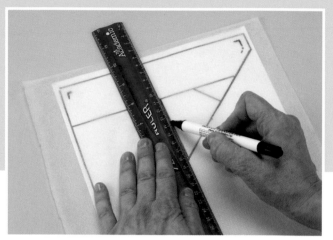

2 Trace the stitching lines within the body of the block using an old ruler (trust me, you don't want ink on your good cutting rulers). If a line extends to the exterior of the block, continue the line out to the cutting line (see step 3).

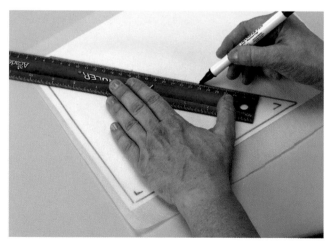

3 Measure out ¼" from the reference corner. This is the cutting line. Trace the entire line around the perimeter of the block. We do this for two reasons: (1) so that the stitching line won't show through the finished quilt block, and (2) to allow fudge room for the block. We'll get to that later when we square up the blocks.

A Note About Using Your Iron-On Pen

Be sure to shake your iron-on transfer pen vigorously before you start to trace. Also have a scrap piece of paper handy to practice before you start tracing. Because the tip needs to be depressed to get the ink flowing, press the tip down gently on the scrap paper until the ink starts to flow. Practice drawing a few lines to see how much pressure you need to apply to get the line size you desire. The thicker the line the more you will see it, but this also increases the chance of the line showing through the finished quilt.

4A The pattern you are using dictates what you will use to trace. If the design is a single block, like design A, use pencil or pen, depending on your eyesight. Make the line dark enough for your eye to see easily.

4B If, like design B, the design has a repeating block that needs to end up facing the same direction in every block, use a Sulky Iron-On Transfer Pen to trace the design onto a blank sheet of paper. Then heat-transfer multiple copies of the pattern onto the foundation fabric. Remember: Before you trace the design, you will need to reverse it since the heat transfer process produces a mirror image of the design. (See page 15.)

4C If, like design C, your pattern doesn't require each repeating block to be oriented in the same direction, use a heat transfer pen to trace the design directly onto the foundation fabric without reversing the design first. You can then use the traced foundation for a block after you heat-transfer the copies, which will be mirror images.

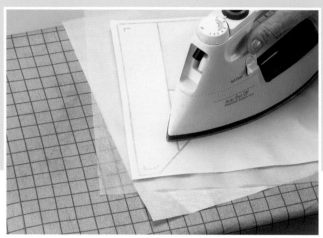 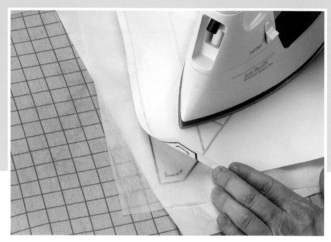

5 Lay the sheet or pressing cloth on the ironing board (the sheet protects your ironing board from any wayward ink) and heat it up a bit. Next lay the foundation block you are going to transfer the design to. Run the iron over it to warm it. Place the traced design ink side down on top of the block and press down (not back and forth) to transfer the design.

Be patient. It takes just a bit to warm up the ink to transfer it. I leave my iron on the cotton setting and don't have any scorching issues. However, your iron may be different. You may want to try it on a lower setting and see if that is hot enough to transfer the design.

6 The longer you leave the iron down, the darker the transferred design will be. But do not set the iron down on the foundation fabric and go check on the cookies in the oven; that will create a problem.

Once the ink and the ironing board are toasty, the transfers will go much quicker. Keep transferring until the ink is too light to see easily. Retrace the lines on the foundation pattern, and resume the transferring! Stack the transferred designs with the ink side up—this is important!

7 Grab a regular pen (do *not* use an iron-on pen!) and write "read me" on one of the outer edges of all of the transfers—remember the ink side is up. Please don't try to figure this out right now; you'll just get a headache. Just trust me and know that I will explain it in due time.

Don't skip this step. If you do, I will not be held accountable for any stress you may encounter on the rest of the journey. Also write "read me" on the original foundation pattern if you are going to use it for a block.

Now that you've done all of the tedious work, it's time to have some fun!

How Do I Get My Fabric Ready?

Most paper-piecing patterns assume you will be using chunks and hunks of fabric. That is a nerve-wracking method for me; I like to work with strips. The designs in this book have measurements in each section that indicate what strip size you need to cover that section. Doesn't that make it easy?

The cutting directions let you know how many strips of each size you need. Your own sewing habits may alter those numbers a bit, but they are good guidelines to start with.

Because the blocks will have all of the seam allowances enclosed, I often rip my strips instead of cutting them. I find that this saves me time, and I enjoy the sound and motion. If you come across a fabric that suffers too much when ripped, just resort to cutting for that particular fabric. Batiks, silks and most cottons rip beautifully. Not only will you save time, but you will also get some exercise and relieve stress with every rip! Because I am lazy, I like to fold the fabric in half, selvage to selvage, and snip the fold. Then I only have to rip half as far! Whoo-hoo!

If the thought of all of this ripping makes you nervous, then by all means cut your strips. Quilting is about joy for you, not adhering to one person's idea of how things are done.

Working With Fabric Strips
I find that working with strips of fabric is far easier than using hunks.

Ripping Versus Cutting
Ripping strips can save you valuable time, but sometimes you come across a fabric that doesn't tear well. That doesn't mean it isn't quality fabric, but too much of the edge is sacrificed by ripping. If this is the case, just rotary cut that fabric.

Now What Do I Do?

The following five rules are stepping stones to successful, fun and stress-free foundation piecing. Don't try to completely understand them right away. Just read them and let them simmer.

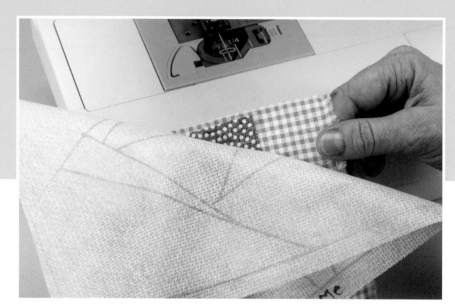

1 Always Sew Through Three Layers
With this technique, you always sew through three layers (two layers of fabric—right sides together—beneath the foundation), not the traditional two.

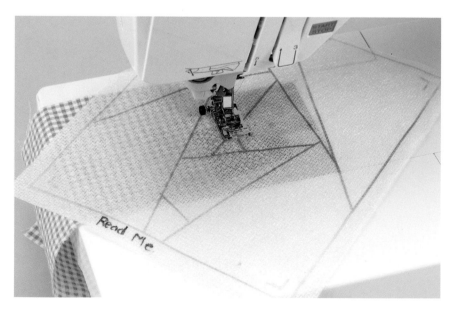

2 "Read Me"
Because we have taken all the time to trace the design on the foundation fabric, we need to keep the foundation on top so we can "read me" while we sew. When you add fabrics to cover the first area, the fabric goes under the foundation.

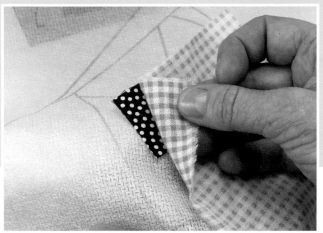

3 "Pretty" Side Out on Number 1

As with traditional quilting, the rights sides of the fabric need to face each other while the wrong sides face out. There is an exception that happens only with piece number 1—it is briefly "pretty" side out. That is, not *up* but *out*. Since the foundation is on top and we slide the first fabric under the foundation, the "pretty" side of the fabric is facing out and down. You can briefly see it before piece number 2 is in place.

4 Number 2 Kisses Number 1

As it is with all pretty things, there is an attraction between the pieces. Piece number 2 "kisses" piece number 1 as it takes its place—right sides together. No kissing the back of the head on this step; it is front to front, right on the lips.

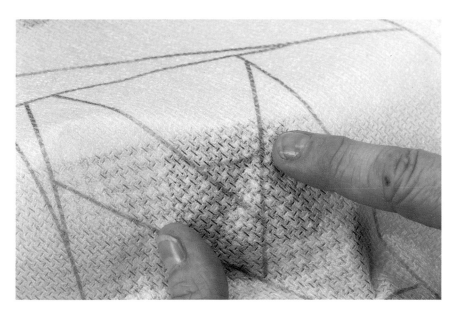

5 Only the Seam Allowance Goes Into the Piece You Add

This step involves leaving your brain outside and just looking at the picture. When piece number 1 and piece number 2 are in place and ready to be sewn, only the seam allowances are in the piece being added. Remember that piece number 1 was "pretty" side out and we are adding piece number 2. The section numbered 2 is not covered by the fabric we are adding for piece number 2. Only the seam allowances are sticking into it.

How Do I Stitch?

In order to make stitching second nature and to reduce brain strain, you can follow certain steps to eliminate the need to think or calculate. You like this already, don't you? Do not try to think about these steps as you read them. Remember: No thinking allowed. Just read the following steps in preparation for further instruction.

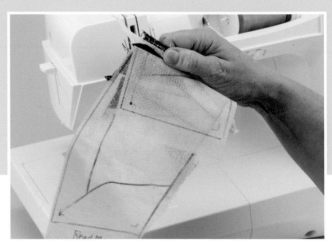

1 Sew From Point A to Point B

In this method, you stitch from the beginning of one line to the end of that line. You do not turn, bend, curve or backstitch. See how easy this is? Stitch from point A to point B and never negotiate a turn.

2 Grab and Shake

After stitching a seam, grab the seam allowances and shake. Not only does this help the fabrics fall away from the seam, it provides exercise as well! Get your whole body into it and shake!

3 Trim and Flip

Lay the block down with the foundation up and still folded back away from the seam allowance. We sew with the foundation up and we cut with the foundation up. Remember all of that time you took to trace the design? You don't want to accidentally cut the foundation, so keep it on top where you can see it. Using the Add-A-Quarter ruler, trim the seam allowance to a neat ¼". If you work with high-contrast fabric, like I do, this step is critical to prevent a very dark fabric from creeping out past the seam allowance in the finished quilt. Often, if I am using a very, very light background, I will trim the dark fabric just a bit narrower than the light fabric. That gives a smidge more protection from show-through. After trimming, flip the block over so that the fabric is right side up and opened flat.

4 Press Fabrics Open

Finger press or use a wooden or plastic iron to open the fabrics. Typically in quilting we talk about pressing the seam allowances open or to one side. That is not the case with this method. We press open the fabrics and do nothing with the seam allowances. They are captured in between the fabric and foundation and are not an issue.

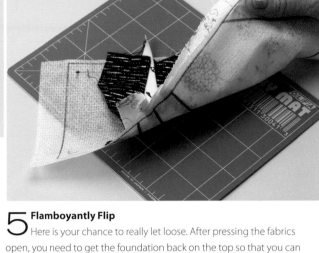

5 Flamboyantly Flip

Here is your chance to really let loose. After pressing the fabrics open, you need to get the foundation back on the top so that you can cut in the next step. This is not a simple flip function. Use artistic flair to flamboyantly flip the block over to lay facedown on the cutting mat. Once again you have an opportunity for exercise in this method. Don't be afraid to experiment and throw in a turn or pirouette while flipping.

6 Count to Identify

An easy way to keep track of where you are and what you need to do next is to count from piece number 1 to the next empty spot. Between that empty spot and the last fabric you added is the next seam to be sewn.

7 Fold and Pretrim

Fold back the foundation right on that seam line. If you prefer a crisper line, fold the foundation against an index card or stiff white paper to create a straighter crease. This can also help you see the traced line on the foundation. Using the Add-A-Quarter ruler, pretrim the ¼" seam allowance on the last piece you added. This pretrimmed edge will provide a guideline for placing the next fabric.

 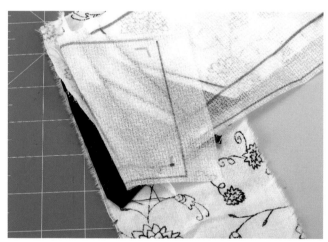

8 Don't Move!

This step is critical. As quilters, we love to pick up our in-process blocks and admire our work. In traditional piecing that is fine. With this method it is deadly. As soon as you pick up the block you'll lose track of where you are and what you should do next. Do not move the block except to gingerly pick up one edge in order to slide the next fabric underneath.

9 Slide and Kiss

You took the time in step 6 to pretrim the edge of the last piece you added; now use that edge. Slide the next fabric underneath, right sides together, and match the edges. You don't need to think about where to place the next piece; the seam allowance is already there as a gauge.

10 Check the Perimeter

This step is one of the most important treasures in this whole book. Mastering this step will alleviate headaches and "oopses" later on in your piecing. Without moving the layered block, identify the corners of the next piece you are adding. Put your finger on one corner of the perimeter and peel back all except the very bottom layer (the fabric you are adding). If there is at least ¼" past your finger, there will be enough fabric to cover the section. Repeat this process, checking each corner of the perimeter to ensure that the fabric you add is large enough to cover the entire section. If one corner comes up short (left), reposition the bottom fabric and check the perimeter again (right).

11 Unfold, and Go Again

When the perimeter has been checked and the coast is clear, unfold the foundation—you are ready to return to step 1 and sew the next seam! Following this progression numerous times will cement it in your memory, and you will zip through those foundation blocks. Don't be frustrated if you need to review the steps; that is the only way you will learn the process! It may be helpful for you to post the steps near your cutting mat. Remember, no stress!

How Do I Finish the Blocks?

When all of the blocks for the quilt are finished, you will move to the ironing board and give them all a press. If you press each block as soon as you finish it, that will take longer! If you wait until they are all finished to do any pressing, you will save all the time it takes to get up and walk to the ironing board and then walk back to your sewing machine a number of times. While this would provide exercise, I think the Flamboyant Flipping (page 27) covers that.

Another temptation is to square up each block as you make it. I don't recommend that either. If you wait until all the block parts are completed, you can measure them and eke out a bit bigger block if you wish.

In that same vein, I recommend trimming on the cutting line of only those seams that are to be joined in multiple-section blocks. Theoretically, the blocks will go together without a hitch and create a block that's just the right size when you seam the sections together.

However, theory and practice can be vastly different. Seam width, fabric bulk, accuracy of traced lines and other factors can come into play and skew a block. If you refrain from cutting on the outside cutting lines (those not joined in seams), you will have more play room to eke out a block that's the correct size, if need be.

Now I'll tell you why the outside stitching lines do not get traced on the foundations: If you trace that line, you are locked into that block size. If you use a very light fabric and try to enlarge the block, the line may show through the finished block. That potential of the line showing through prevents making the block a little bigger than the pattern even if you have the extra fabric on the outside to work with. That is an opportunity wasted.

However, the most important reason is that it gives you "fudge" room. By omitting that line, you provide ¼" without any restrictive lines on each side of a block. That equals ½" of room to shift the block if need be. That is a lot of fudge!

Pressing the Blocks

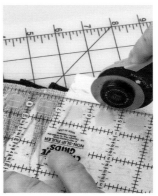

Trimming Recommendations

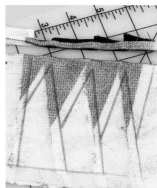

Resisting the Urge to Cut

Extra Fabric (the Fudge Factor)

Chart a Course for Success

At the end of each one of my workshops, students leave with these charts to help them remember the key ideas. What are the key elements to look for in fabric? What features matter when it comes to the foundation? How does the whole thing work, again? That's a lot to remember, so these charts gather the basic ideas to help jog your memory. Keep them nearby as you work through the projects.

But there's one thing you need to remember always: *Mistake* is not a word we use. We only have *opportunities*!

Before You Start:

1 Always sew through 3 layers.

2 "Read me."

3 "Pretty" side out on number 1.

4 Number 2 kisses number 1.

5 ONLY the seam allowance goes into the piece you add.

Stitching:

1 Point A to Point B

2 Grab and Shake

3 Trim and Flip

4 Press Fabrics Open

5 Flamboyantly Flip

6 Count to Identify

7 Fold and Pretrim

8 Don't Move!

9 Slide and Kiss

10 Check the Perimeter

11 Unfold, and Go Again

Fabric Choices:

SCALE

CONTRAST

VALUE

That is all you need to know!

Foundation Choices:

Can I see through it?

Can I iron it?

Is it strong?

Is it washable?

What Do I Make?

Now it is time to decide what to make! The projects are arranged to help you build confidence, and then let you soar! Keep your chart nearby, and let's get started.

The first two quilts are "Easiest." Try one or both, and once you are comfortable foundation piecing large blocks, move to slightly smaller, one-unit "Easier" blocks.

All five of the subsequent quilts are "Easy" quilts, with two-unit blocks. You won't even have broken a sweat when you start tackling the "Still Easy" projects. After trying your hand at the multiple blocks, smaller pieces, and additional techniques, embark on the "Not Hard" quilts. Even if the quilts in this section seem difficult due to their subject matter, or maybe the pieces seem tiny—don't discount them. By the time you reach the end, it'll be a no-stress breeze. No more hives and no more tweezers. Life is truly good!

Simple Pine

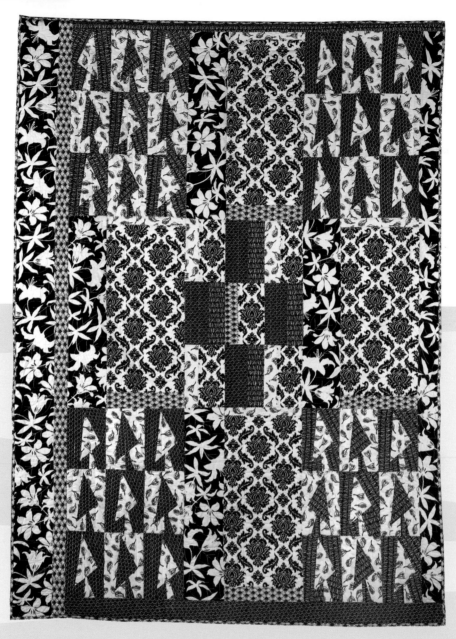

Are you ready to start this foundation-piecing adventure? Pick out some luscious fabrics, and I'll walk you through the rest. This first lesson could be a single-block pot holder, but that's pishposh! We can do more than that! I guarantee you'll want to make more than one block. Why? The block is simple, and the quilt is simply sensational!

Just what is a *Simple Pine*? I checked one dictionary and found eleven definitions for *simple*. Does that make it an oxymoron? Out of those offerings, I like "guileless" the best. These pines rest amid one of the most unpretentious blocks in quilting. Set in a nine-patch, the values alternate and play as the chipmunks do in the forest.

Not only are the pines set in a nine-patch, but the entire quilt is a nine-patch bordered asymmetrically. Straightforward and trouble-free, this first adventure into *stress-free* foundation piecing offers an opportunity to take a foundation-piecing journey and wind up with a significant quilt when you're done. No pot holder exercise for us!

Simple Pine
Finished Quilt: 65½"×86"
Pieced and quilted by the author
Fabrics courtesy of Joel Dewberry for Westminster Fibers

materials

Medium dark value, black with ecru, large-scale floral print: 2½ yards

Medium light, ecru with black, large-scale wallpaper print: 1¾ yards

Medium light, ecru with black, medium-scale print: 2 yards

Medium dark value, black with ecru, basket print: 1¾ yards

Medium dark value, black with ecru, twig print: 1⅝ yards

Medium value, ecru with black and red, basket print: 1 yard

Foundation Fabric: 7 yards of 12" wide foundation

Backing: 5¼ yards

Batting: 72½" × 94"

Sulky Iron-On Transfer Pen

Fabric Suggestions

Grab the biggest, boldest print you can find for the borders and the four blocks. Vary the value a bit so they have some contrast.

For the trees, choose two dark fabrics that differ in pattern but are nearly identical in value (below). The basket weave complements the more contemporary twig print, and they both maintain their personality instead of blending.

Unlike most of my quilts, the zinger in this piece (the red basket print) isn't as dominant. Because of the ensemble feel of the quilt, I didn't want to upset the fluidity. No fabric is the star, but they all deserve an Oscar!

cutting list

Strips are cut across the width of the fabric unless otherwise stated.

From floral print:
    Cut 7 strips 6½" for Left Border and blocks, then from these strips cut the following:
        4 strips 6½" × 27½" for Alternating Block
    Cut 2 strips 3½" for Right Border

From wallpaper print:
    Cut 4 strips 12½" , then from these strips cut the following:
        4 strips 12½" × 23¾"
    Cut 2 strips 4½", then from these strips cut the following
        5 strips 4½" × 9½" for Center Block

From ecru, medium-scale print:
    Cut 1 strip 2½" , then from this strip cut the following:
        4 strips 2½" × 9½" for Center Block
    Cut 2 strips 1¾", then from this strip cut the following:
        4 strips 1¾" × 12½" for Alternating Block

    Cut 3 strips 6" for 9-Patch Pine Blocks
    Cut 4 strips 4" for 9-Patch Pine Blocks
    Cut 4 strips 3½" for 9-Patch Pine Blocks
    Cut 3 strips 3" for 9-Patch Pine Blocks
    Cut 3 strips 2½" for 9-Patch Pine Blocks

From black basket print:
    Cut 1 strip 4", then from this strip cut the following:
        4 strips 4" × 9 ½" for Center Block
    Cut 2 strips 3½" for Bottom Border
    Cut 2 strips 6" for 9-Patch Pine Blocks
    Cut 3 strips 4" for 9-Patch Pine Blocks
    Cut 3 strips 3½" for 9-Patch Pine Blocks
    Cut 2 strips 3" for 9-Patch Pine Blocks
    Cut 2 strips 2½" for 9-Patch Pine Blocks

From twig print:
    Cut 1 strip 3", then from this strip cut the following:
        4 strips 3" × 9½" for Center Block
    Cut 2 strips 2" for Top Border
    Cut 2 strips 6" for 9-Patch Pine Blocks
    Cut 3 strips 4" for 9-Patch Pine Blocks
    Cut 3 strips 3½" for 9-Patch Pine Blocks
    Cut 3 strips 3" for 9-Patch Pine Blocks
    Cut 2 strips 2½" for 9-Patch Pine Blocks

From red basket print:
    Cut 2 strips 3" for piecing, then from this strip cut the following:
        4 strips 3" × 12½" for Alternating Block
    Cut 4 strips 2½", then from one of these strips cut the following:
        1 strip 2½" × 9½" for Center Block
    Cut 8 strips 2¼" for binding

From foundation fabric:
    Cut 36 rectangles approximately 7" × 10"

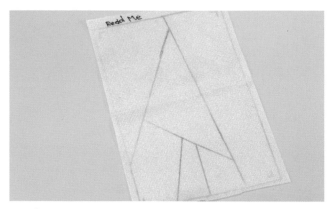

Simple Pine 1

Simple Pine 2

Simple Pine 3

Preparation

1 Hide all strips cut for the regular piecing of the blocks and borders. The rest of the strips will be used for foundation piecing, and we don't want to accidentally use a strip we need later.

2 Using the iron-on transfer pen, trace 1 copy of the Simple Pine pattern onto a 7" × 10" foundation rectangle.

3 Use this tracing to heat-transfer Simple Pine onto the other 35 foundation rectangles (Simple Pine 1). When the lines start to get faint, remember to retrace the lines, then keep transferring!

Piecing the Pines

1 Piece your first tree with the black twig print for the tree and the ecru, medium-scale print for the background. (Do not mix the black twig print and the black basket print together. Use only 1 dark print per tree.) Follow the foundation pattern to guide you on strip width and fabric placement.

2 Continue piecing to make a total of 8 dark trees with the black twig print.

3 Switch gears, and piece a total of 10 light trees (using the ecru, medium scale print) with the light background (using the black twig print).

4 Repeat this process with the black basket fabric, making a total of 10 light trees and 8 dark trees.

5 When all 36 trees have been pieced, press them well.

6 Square each tree to 6½" × 9½", being careful to keep points intact. I can never remember if I should trim branches in spring or fall, so let's not trim any!

Creating the 9-Patch

1 Gather the pines in 2 stacks, light trees in 1 pile on the left and the dark trees on the right (Simple Pine 5). Separate the black twig print trees from the black basket print trees. Use only 1 black print in each 9-patch block. Make two 9-patches with each fabric

2 Flip 1 dark tree over onto 1 light tree so that their right sides face each other, and stitch them together (Simple Pine 6). Stitch a total of 12 pairs in this manner. Make sure to match the blocks with like black fabric.

3 Add 1 light tree on the right side of each of the first 8 pairs to make the top and bottom rows of the 9-patch blocks. This will give you a total of 8 rows that have 2 light trees surrounding 1 dark tree.

4 To each of the 4 remaining pairs, add 1 dark tree to the left side of the pair. These are the middle row of the 9-patch blocks

5 Press all the seams toward the dark blocks.

6 To build one 9-patch block, sew a row from step 3 to the top of a row from step 4, then sew another row from step 3 to the bottom. Make a total of 4 of these 9-patch blocks. Make a total of 2 blocks from each black print and press.

Creating the Center Block

1 Find the strips you hid from yourself during preparation. Stitch an ecru, medium-scale 2½" × 9½" strip onto the left side of a 4½" × 9½" wallpaper print strip. Make a total of 4 of these blocks, and press the seams toward the wallpaper print.

2 Stitch the red basket print 2½" × 9½" strip onto the left side of the remaining 4½" × 9½" wallpaper print strip. Press the seam toward the wallpaper print.

3 Stitch a 3" × 9½" twig print strip onto the right side of a 4" × 9½" black basket print strip. Repeat to make all 4 sets. Press the seams toward the black basket print strip.

4 Following the center block diagram (Simple Pine 8), sew the 9 sets from steps 1–3 into 3 rows. Press the seams toward the black blocks.

5 Stitch the 3 rows together to make the center block.

Simple Pine 5

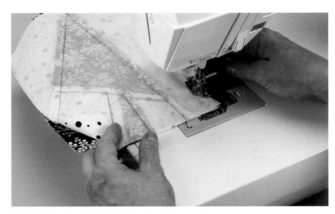

Simple Pine 6

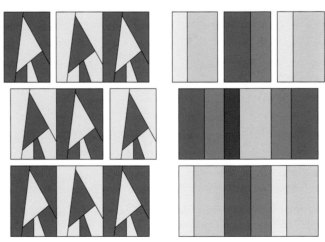

Simple Pine 7   Simple Pine 8

Simple Pine 9

Creating the Alternating Block

1 Stitch a 1¾" × 12½" ecru, medium-scale strip on the top of a 12½" × 23¾" wallpaper print strip, and press the seam up toward the twig strip. Repeat to make a total of 4 units.

2 Stitch a 3" × 12½" red basket print strip to the bottom of each of the 4 units from step 1. Press the seams down.

3 Finish each block by sewing a 6½" × 27½" floral strip to the left side. Press the seams out toward the floral strip.

Creating the Top

1 Sew an alternating block to the right of a 9-patch tree block made with the black twig print. Sew a basket print 9-patch tree block to the right side of the alternating block, and press the seams toward the alternating block. This is Row 1.

2 Sew an alternating block to the right side of a basket print 9-patch block. Sew a twig print 9-patch to the right side of the alternating block. Press the seams toward the alternating block. This is Row 3.

3 Sew the center block in between 2 alternating blocks, and press the seams toward the alternating blocks. This is Row 2.

4 Join all 3 rows in order from top to bottom to make the 9-patch quilt center. Press the seams.

Simple Pine 10

Adding the Borders

1 Remove the selvages from the 3½" floral strips, and stitch the strips together end to end. Press the seam open. From this, cut a border strip 3½" × 81½", and stitch it to the right-hand side of the quilt. Press the seam out.

2 Remove the selvages from the 3½" black basket print strips, and stitch the strips together end to end. Press the seam open. From this, cut a border strip 3½" × 57½", and stitch it to the bottom of the quilt. Press the seam out.

3 Remove the selvages from the 2" twig print strips, and stitch the strips together end to end. Press the seam open. From this, cut a border strip 2" × 57½". Stitch to the top of the quilt. Press the seam out.

4 Remove the selvages from 3 of the 2½" red basket print strips, and stitch them together end to end. Press the seams open.

5 Remove the selvages from the 6½" floral strips, and stitch the strips together end to end. Press the seams open.

6 Stitch the red basket print strip from step 4 to the right-hand side of the large floral strip from step 5. Press the seam toward the floral strip.

7 From the unit from step 6, cut a border strip (from both borders at once, no less!) 86" long. Stitch this border unit to the left side of the quilt. Press the seam out.

8 Can you believe your first foundation-piecing experience was this easy and fun? Whoo-hoo!

Simple Pine 11

Simple Pine 12

Simple Pine 13

Simple Pine 14

Layering, Quilting and Binding

1 The fabrics in this quilt are so busy and prominent that they truly don't need much quilting. To surprise the evergreens on the quilt, I put quilted leaves anywhere the large floral print appears in the quilt. The width of the strip dictated the size of the leaves.

2 I found it best to follow the wallpaper print's lead. I quilted a loose serpentine connecting the diagonal elements in the print and then overlapped a grid to hold the print down a bit more.

3 The trees are stretched vertically with straight-line quilting throughout the 9-patch stand blocks.

4 I emphasized the non-zinger zinger with a serpentine stitch for added texture.

5 And there you have the simply quilted *Simple Pines*. Congratulations—you did it!

Are We There Yet?

When I think of traditional Amish quilts, my mind turns to the Flying Geese quilts in those rich, dark and simple colors. The clean lines and high contrast appeal to my eye, but I can't help but wish they were a little less symmetrical! Symmetry has never been a dear friend of mine.

In this project quilt, the orderly arrangement wobbles and shifts from the methodical "V" of flying geese to the stretch of tall pines toward light.

The wonky equilibrium mirrors long lines of bellowing geese as they cut through the evening sky. How do they know where they are going? Do they have a compass loaded on a wing tip? I certainly do better navigating with a compass on my windshield...

However they do it, it totally amazes me! I fantasize about the families traveling together as they fly over in formation. Line shuffling abounds as siblings bicker and get sent back in line by a "road weary" parent. After a few reorganizations without the desired result, papa squawks, "Don't make me pull over!" The baby of the family cries, "He's touching me!" while the oldest sibling orders, "Stay out of my spot. Don't cross that line!" Momentary silence, and then momma is asked yet again, "*Are We There Yet?*"

Some things are universal.

Are We There Yet?

Finished Quilt 39½" × 52"
Pieced and quilted by the author

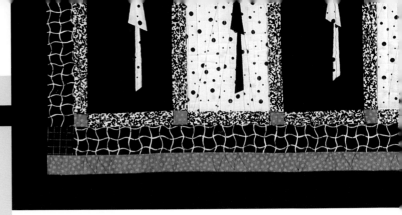

materials

Outer Border Fabric: 1 yard large-scale black-on-black grid print

Inner Border Fabric: ⅜ yard medium-scale dark black with white grid print

Inner Border Cornerstone Fabric: ⅛ yard dark black plaid

Zinger Cornerstone and Anchor Border Fabric: ¼ yard green polka-dot print

Light Fabric: 1½ yards white with black polka-dot print

Dark Fabric: ¼ yard of 8 different medium- and small-scale black-on-black prints

Lattice Fabric: ⅜ yard medium white with black pixel print

Binding Fabric: ⅔ yard dark black with white plaid

Foundation Fabric: 3 ⅛ yards of 12" wide foundation

Backing Fabric: 1 ⅝ yards white-on-white print

Batting: Crib size

Sulky Iron-On Transfer Pen

Fabric Suggestions

I used eight black fabrics that look alike from a few feet away. But when you approach the quilt, the subtleties of texture are a wonderful surprise.

The cornerstone and anchor border should really pop while the lattice print should be a bridge between light and dark fabrics.

cutting list

Strips are cut across the width of the fabric unless otherwise stated.

From Outer Border Fabric:
Cut 1 strip 6½", then from this strip cut the following:
    1 strip 6½" × 39½"
Cut 3 strips 5", then from these strips cut the following:
    2 strips 5" × 41½"
    1 strip 5" × 39½"

From Inner Border Fabric:
Cut 4 strips 2", then from these strips cut the following:
    2 strips 2" × 37½"
    2 strips 2" × 27½"

From Inner Border Cornerstone Fabric:
Cut 1 strip 2", then from this strip cut the following:
    4 squares 2" × 2"

From Zinger Cornerstone and Anchor Border Fabric:
Cut 1 strip 1¼" for Zinger Cornerstones, then from this strip cut the following:
    12 squares 1¼" × 1¼"
Cut 1 strip 1½" for the Anchor Border, then from this strip cut the following:
    1 strip 1½" × 30½"

From Light Fabric for "Trees":
Cut 3 strips 3½"
Cut 5 strips 3"
Cut 4 strips 2½"
Cut 2 strips 2"

From Dark Fabric for "Trees":
Cut 3 strips 3½"
Cut 5 strips 3"
Cut 4 strips 2½"
Cut 2 strips 2"

From Lattice Fabric:
Cut 7 strips 1¼", then from these strips cut the following:
    6 strips 1¼" × 36"
    10 strips 1¼" × 5"

From Binding Fabric:
Cut 1 square to make 2¼" continuous bias binding

From Foundation Fabric:
Cut 5 strips 5½" × 36½"

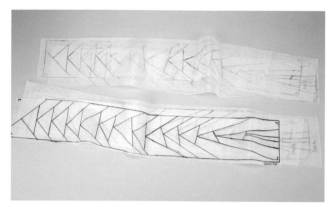

Are We There Yet? 1

Are We There Yet? 2

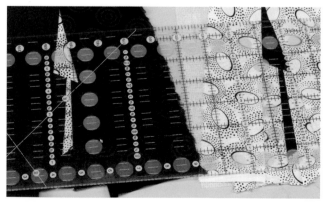

Are We There Yet? 3

Are We There Yet? 4

Preparation

1 From the foundation fabric, cut five 5½" × 36½" strips.

2 Using an iron-on transfer pen, trace 1 copy of the tree onto 1 of the 5½" × 36½" strips from step 1. Tracing right on the foundation fabric and then using *that* for the transfer and a foundation piece will make that tree the reverse of the others, as in my quilt.

3 Place the traced tree pattern facedown on another foundation strip from step 1, and heat-transfer the design by pressing. If the ink becomes too faint, retrace the existing lines on the pattern and try it again! Repeat this process to make a total of 5 foundations, including the traced foundation from step 2 (Are We There Yet? 1).

Piecing the Trees

1 Separate the 5 foundations into 2 piles. The pile with 2 foundations will be pieced with dark "trees," and the pile with 3 foundations will be pieced with light "trees."

2 Piece 2 strips with dark trees and a light background (Are We There Yet? 2).

3 Piece 3 strips with light trees and a dark background (Are We There Yet? 3).

4 Press all 5 tree strips.

5 With the foundation fabric up, square each tree strip to 5" × 36". Keeping the foundation side up helps you trim the trees without losing any branches! You can vary the placement of the trees in this step by leaving more background on the bottom of some of the strips (Are We There Yet? 4). That small variation will add interest.

6 Alternate the trees by value on a design wall (simply use a piece of batting or the back side of a vinyl tablecloth taped to the wall).

Assembling the Quilt Center Rows

1 Sew a 1¼" × 36" lattice strip to the right-hand side of each tree strip.

2 Press the seam allowance toward the lattice strip.

3 Sew the remaining 1¼" × 36" lattice strip to the left side of the left-most tree strip.

4 Press the seam allowance toward the lattice strip.

5 Join the tree strips in an alternating pattern. Make sure that the tree strip from step 3 stays on the far left.

6 Press the seam allowances toward the lattice strips.

Framing the Quilt Center With Lattice

1 Sew 1 zinger cornerstone to 1 end of each of the 1¼" × 5" lattice strips. Sew a second zinger cornerstone to the opposite end of 2 of the strips (Are We There Yet? 5).

2 Press the seam allowances toward the lattice strips.

3 Using 1 strip with 2 zinger cornerstones as a starting point, build an entire lattice strip by adding 4 of the lattice strips that have 1 cornerstone. Attach the strips end to end to make 1 long strip of 6 cornerstones with 5 lattice strips (Are We There Yet? 6).

4 Repeat step 3 to make a second long lattice strip. Press the seam allowances of both long lattice strips toward the lattice fabric.

5 Stitch 1 long lattice strip to the top of the quilt center and the other long lattice strip to the bottom of the quilt center. Press the seam allowances out toward the long lattice strip.

Assembling the Top

1 Sew a 2" inner border cornerstone to each end of both of the 2" × 27½" inner border strips. Press the seam allowances toward the strips.

2 Sew the 2" × 37½" inner border strips to the sides of the quilt center. Press the seam allowances out toward the border strips.

3 Sew the inner border plus cornerstone strips (from step 1) to the top and bottom of the quilt center. Press the seam allowances out toward the borders.

4 Stitch the 1½" × 30½" anchor border strip to the bottom of the quilt, and press the seam allowance out toward the anchor border.

5 Stitch the 5" × 41½" outer border strips to the sides of the quilt, and press the seam allowances out toward the outer borders.

6 Stitch the 5" × 39½" outer border strip to the top of the quilt, and press the seam allowance out toward the outer border. Then stitch the 6½" × 39½" outer border strip to the bottom of the quilt, and press the seam allowance out toward the outer border.

Finishing the Goodies

1 The quilting in this piece is secondary to the actual piecing. Stitching in the ditch would work to outline the shapes and lattice grid. Vertical lines throughout the quilt would also work.

2 The graphic center of this quilt holds the story. I just tried not to disturb it with disruptive or unruly quilting.

Are We There Yet? 5

Are We There Yet? 6

Are We There Yet? 7

Tall Pines

The fabric inspiration for this quilt came from an unlikely source: my non-quilting sister! Jill was at a show with me and spied the lovely fabric in the border. She thought I might like it. Of course I do! The calm, elegant characters brought to mind a tranquil stand of pines. The wind whispers through the needles, and the spent ones carpet the forest floor. The smell and the stillness of that image flood me with calm and peace. My idyllic childhood memories are infused with those smells and sounds from Wisconsin summers. What better way to get centered and calm than by recalling joy and serenity in one fell swoop? Just looking at *Tall Pines* takes me through fabulous summer adventures and evokes a fond memory of a perfect gift. Breathe in the earthy fragrance, and start on your own journey of "peacing" a quilt.

Tall Pines

Finished Quilt: 34" × 77"
Pieced and quilted by the author

materials

Background Fabric: 2¼ yards

Insert Panel Fabric: ¾ yard

Pine Fabric: ¾ yard

Cornerstone Fabric: ⅛ yard

Lattice Fabric: ½ yard

Border Fabric: 1 yard

Binding Fabric: ¾ yard

Foundation Fabric: 5 yards of 12" wide foundation

Batting: 42" × 85"

Backing: 2¼ yards

Sulky Iron-On Transfer Pen

Fabric Suggestions

This quilt was driven by the fabulous fabric. Find that inspiring material for yourself, and build from there. It is critical that you love the border and the insert fabric. Don't be satisfied until you find exactly what makes you sigh.

The cornerstone in the piece is not so much a zinger as a semicolon. It causes the eyes to rest, but it doesn't grab focus as the zinger normally does. Choose a complementary piece that highlights your fabulous print but doesn't dominate it.

Because the blocks are large, a lot of the background is seen. Select for the background a fabric that is interesting and not flat in appearance, unless you are going for the stark contrast of pristine white with strong black trees.

cutting list

Strips are cut across the width of the fabric unless otherwise stated.

From Background Fabric:
    Cut an assortment of strips 4", 6" and 8"

From Insert Panel Fabric:
    Cut 2 strips 8½", then from these strips cut the following:
        2 strips 8½" × 24½"

From Pine Fabric:
    Cut an assortment of strips 3" and 4"

From Cornerstone Fabric:
    Cut 1 strip 1¼", then from this strip cut the following:
        12 squares 1¼" × 1¼"

From Lattice Fabric:
    Cut 7 strips 1¼", then from these strips cut the following:
        6 strips 1¼" × 24½"
        6 strips 1¼" × 16½"
        4 strips 1¼" × 8½"

From Border Fabric:
    Cut 6 strips 4½"

From Binding Fabric:
    Cut 1 square 23" × 23" to make 2¼" bias binding

From Foundation Fabric:
    Cut 12 rectangles 17" × 7"

Tall Pines 1

Tall Pines 2

Preparation

1 Trace each pine tree with an iron-on transfer pen onto 1 foundation rectangle. Heat-transfer 1 tree onto each of the remaining foundation rectangles for a total of 12.

2 Make 2¼" continual bias binding (Tall Pines 1). I like to prepare the binding at this stage so that it is ready and waiting. When I'm done with the top and the quilting, I'm so excited to see the binding ready to be slapped on!

Piecing the Tall Pines

1 Foundation piece the 12 tall pine blocks according to the fabric key and the numerical sequence on the foundation pattern. Press the blocks.

2 With the foundation up, square each block to 6½" × 16½". Make sure you preserve those pine points! Keep your quilt free of bruised branches.

Building the Stand of Pines

1 Arrange the pines in 3 stands of 4 pines each. When you are pleased with the arrangement of your 3 stands of pines, sew the blocks together to form 3 rows. Press the seam allowances open.

2 Sew a 1¼" × 24½" lattice piece to the top and to the bottom of each stand. Press each seam allowance toward the lattice.

3 Sew a cornerstone square to each end of a 1¼" × 16½" lattice piece. Repeat for the other five 1¼" × 16½" lattice pieces. Press the seams toward the lattice.

4 Sew the strips from step 3 to each end of each stand. Press the seam allowances out toward the lattice strips.

5 Sew the 1¼" × 8½" lattice strips to each end of the 8½" × 24½" insert panels. Press the seam allowances out toward the lattice strips.

6 Arrange the stands from step 4 on a design wall so that an insert panel is between each pair of stands. When you are pleased with the arrangement, sew the stands to the insert panels to make one quilt center with lattice already attached.

7 Press the seam allowances toward the lattice. You're almost done! It's border time. Take a step back and enjoy your work. Can you smell the pine needles yet?

Adding the Border

1 Trim selvages off of the border strips and sew all 6 of the 4½" strips together end to end into 1 long strip. Press the seams open

2 From the long border strip you sewed in step 1, cut 2 strips 4½" × 69". Sew 1 strip to each side of the quilt. Press the seams out toward the borders.

3 From the rest of the long border strip you sewed in step 1, cut 2 strips 4½" × 34". Sew 1 strip to the top and 1 strip to the bottom of the quilt. Press the seams out toward the borders.

Layering, Quilting and Binding

1 I kept the quilting simple in the insert panels. I wanted a parchment look, so I kept it loose and more puffed out as opposed to the flatter background around the trees.

2 The background has a circular motif that contrasts the angular trees and lets them rise and float above the quilt.

3 The border has such beautiful fabric that I stayed out of its way and just gave it a little texture to keep it lower than the puffy insert panels.

4 Your binding is all ready, so sew it on with a walking foot.

5 Make sure you sign your quilt before you hang it up. Take ownership of your quilt and your peace.

Tall Pines 3

Door Number B

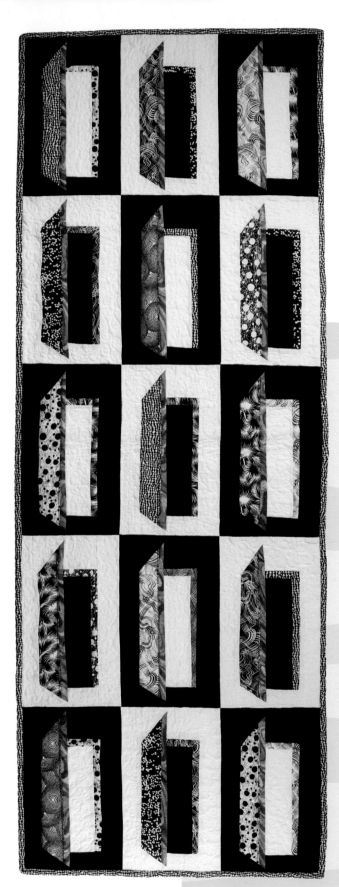

I don't design anything that doesn't have a story thread flowing through my life. Sometimes I visualize myself as one of those pots of paint that get spun to spew colorful splotches onto unsuspecting paper. What are those things called? Anyway, the ideas and life stories spin around inside and burst through the surface as quilts.

This quilt story is about my struggle in life to see the glass as half full. It has often been easier and more comfortable for me to see the negative sides of situations. I could rattle off a whole list of things that were wrong with a situation, but could I see the positive slant? Not very often. But I have discovered that when I remember that my glass is half full, it truly improves my life.

One way to see the good is to focus on traveling forward rather than wallowing in the past. I repeat well-worn but wise proverbs, such as "This too shall pass" or "Look at the big picture." Phrases like these are not to be taken lightly. They have helped me to see the door opening on my future. I'm not agonizing over the road I've traveled; I'm gazing at the horizon and wondering what surprises it holds for today.

This life journey just gets better and better. I see the open door, and while I'm cautious about entering, I intend to fling myself head-long into the wonders on the other side. I'm in awe of the twists and turns my quilts have created in my life. It is marvelous!

I have peeked in the first door. It looks orderly and lovely in there, but where are the slants and wonks and pazowies? The television show *Let's Make a Deal* taught me that choices can be made, and you don't have to settle for what appears first. I admire those that embrace the order and beauty of the first door, but I'm trading it for *Door Number B*! Thanks, Monty Hall!

Door Number B
Finished Quilt: 20" × 56"
Pieced and quilted by the author
Fabrics courtesy of Red Rooster Fabrics

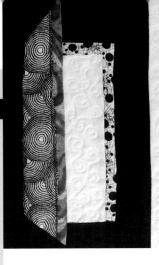

materials

Door and Door Frame Fabric: 8 fat quarters of a mixture of medium light, medium or medium dark black prints in varying scales

Light Background, Inner Door and Backing Fabric: 2¾ yards light value white-on-white print

Dark Background and Inner Door Fabric: ⅞ yard dark value black solid

Zinger Fabric: ¼ yard powerful pink swirl pattern

Binding Fabric: ⅓ yard zippy medium value black check-like print

Foundation Fabric: 5 yards at least 9" wide

Backing: 1¾ yards

Batting: 24" × 60"

1 sheet of white paper 8½" × 11"

Sulky Iron-On Transfer Pen

Fabric Suggestions

Go for the gusto with this design. Contrast is the key, so make the dark really, really dark and the light ultra light.

Just play with medium to medium dark prints for the doors and door frames. Anything goes!

cutting list

Strips are cut across the width of the fabric unless otherwise stated.

From Door and Door Frame Fabric:
    Cut 2 strips 2" from each fat quarter
    Cut 1 strip 1¼" from each fat quarter
    (You may need to cut more later.)

From Light Background and Inner Door Fabric:
    Cut 2 strips 5"
    Cut 2 strips 3½"
    Cut 5 strips 2½", then from these strips cut the following:
        2 strips 2½" × 8"

From Dark Background and Inner Door Fabric:
    Cut 2 strips 5"
    Cut 2 strips 3½"
    Cut 3 strips 2½", then from these strips cut the following:
        7 strips 2½" × 8"

From Zinger Fabric:
    Cut 6 strips 1", then from these strips cut the following:
        15 strips 1" × 11"

From Binding Fabric:
    Cut 1 square 20" × 20" to make 2¼" continuous bias binding

From Foundation Fabric:
    Cut 15 rectangles 7½" × 12"

Door Number B 1

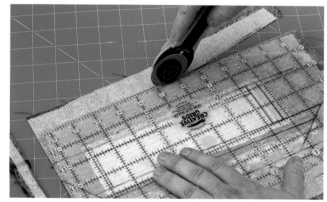

Door Number B 2

Door Number B 3

Preparation

1 Trace the *Door Number B* foundation pattern onto a sheet of white paper with an iron-on transfer pen. Use this paper to heat-transfer the door pattern onto the 15 foundation rectangles.

Piecing the Doors

1 Foundation piece the door blocks according to the numerical sequence on the foundation pattern.

2 Whichever background you choose for the inner door (1 on the foundation pattern), you will use the opposite value for pieces 4, 5, 8, 9, 10, 11 and 12. Use the pictures to help you with fabric placement (Door Number B 1).

3 Piece 8 blocks with the light background for the inner door, and piece 7 blocks with the dark background for the inner door, for a total of 15 blocks.

4 After all blocks are pieced, press them.

5 Square each block to 7" × 11½" (Door Number B 2).

Arranging the Blocks

1 Using a design wall, the floor or a bed, arrange the blocks as shown in the quilt diagram.

2 Sew 3 door blocks together, alternating the values, to make a row. Repeat with the remaining door blocks to make a total of 5 rows.

3 Press the seams toward the door blocks with the dark background.

4 Join the rows—be sure to alternate the background values—to complete the quilt center (Door Number B 3). Press the seams down. Because there are no borders in this quilt, you are already done piecing!

Layering, Quilting and Binding

1 Make 2¼" continuous bias binding and set aside.

2 Quilt in parallel vertical lines along the straight lines of the quilt (Door Number B 4). Or, you can break up the quilting by doing a serpentine line on the lighter values (Door Number B 5).

I wanted the doors to puff out to add texture, so I didn't quilt in those spaces.

3 Bind with a snazzy binding, and you've completed another quilt! Don't forget to add a hanging sleeve. Also add a personalized label, or just sign and date your work.

Door Number B 4

Door Number B 5

Another Idea

Remember, the fabrics chosen and layouts used for this project are just guidelines. There are all sorts of exciting and fun variations or additions.

For example, you might try using all light backgrounds in the inner doors and all dark backgrounds around the doors. This could make a wonderful signature quilt for a new neighbor, an old neighbor, a graduate, a co-worker, a quilting buddy—the list could go on and on! Just use your talents and create a one-of-a-kind gift that the recipient will treasure for a lifetime.

I hope it was worth trading Door Number 1 for Door Number B. If not, see Monty; it is out of my control!

Crooked Cabins

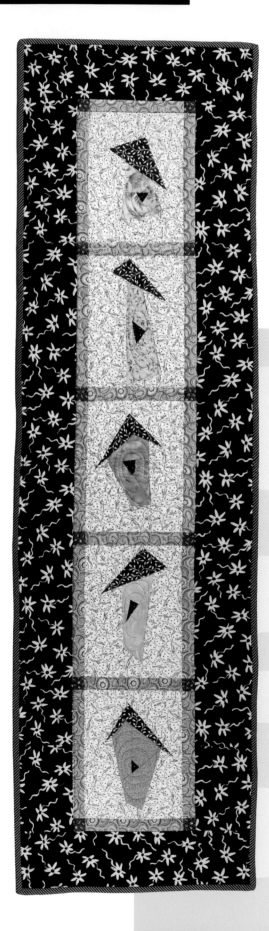

One spring my children and I nursed two very young avian orphans back to health and set them free. These orphans required warmth, safety and some mushed-up cat food. (It seemed odd to feed cat food to baby birds, but I trusted the vet and forged ahead.) Apparently it is quite difficult to save baby birds and then release them to fend for themselves. Not ones to balk at a challenge, we proceeded to feed our little ones, Robinson and Tiny, and change their bedding on a regular basis. And feed and change and feed and change. Newborns are newborns whatever species they are!

Naturally, we became quite attached to our charges and have fond memories of caring for them and teaching them how to survive. I cherish the memory of my children flapping their arms and running in circles to teach the birds to fly! Perched on our fingers, our heads, or our neighbor's head, they never ceased to delight us.

I'm glad my children had an opportunity to practice loving and letting go. It's not an easy lesson for any of us. Both Robinson and Tony independently flew off into their futures. We saw them visit and heard them call after they moved out on their own. Satisfaction.

We now have the reputation as the "Bird Family," so we need to keep accommodations ready and waiting for any orphans that need us. *Crooked Cabins* represents the standing invitation for itty-bitty orphans to find their way into our yard and into our hearts.

Crooked Cabins
Finished Quilt: 15" × 52"
Pieced and quilted by the author

materials

Background Fabric: ½ yard small-scale reproduction white with black print

House Fabric: ⅛ yard each of 5 different pink tone-on-tone prints

Roof Fabric: ⅛ yard medium-scale black with white print

Peephole Fabric: ⅛ yard very dark black

Lattice Fabric: ¼ yard medium-scale, medium-value reproduction print

Cornerstone Fabric: ⅛ yard small-scale, dark-value black reproduction print

Border Fabric: ⅝ yard large-scale, dark-value black with white contemporary print

Binding: ½ yard black with white stripe

Backing: 1¾ yards

Foundation Fabric: 1⅓ yard of 12" wide foundation

Batting: 18½" × 56"

Pencil or pen

Fabric Suggestions

Reproduction fabrics are so fun to mix with contemporary prints. This quilt combines the two for a unique look.

Find a border print that is bold enough to frame the houses yet not overpowering.

Select pinks that are close in color and value but have subtle differences worthy of using that many fabrics! If they are too close, your time spent choosing different fabrics will have been in vain.

cutting list

Strips are cut across the width of the fabric unless otherwise stated.

From Background Fabric:
    Cut 1 strip 7"
    Cut 1 strip 6"

From Roof Fabric:
    Cut 1 strip 3"

From Peephole Fabric:
    Cut 1 strip 2"

From Lattice Fabric:
    Cut 4 strips 1¼", then from these strips, cut the following:
        6 strips 1¼" × 6½"
        10 strips 1¼" × 8½"

From Cornerstone Fabric:
    Cut 1 strip 1¼", then from this strip, cut the following:
        12 squares 1¼" × 1¼"

From Border Fabric:
    Cut 4 strips 4"

From Foundation Fabric:
    Cut 5 rectangles 7" × 9"

From Binding Fabric:
    Cut 1 square 18" x 18" to make 2¼" continuous bias binding

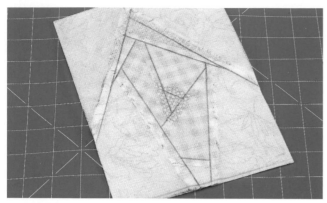

Crooked Cabins 1

Preparation

1 Use a pencil or pen to trace cabin pattern onto each foundation rectangle with a pencil or pen.

Piecing the Cabin Blocks

1 Foundation piece the cabin blocks according to the key and numerical sequence on the foundation pattern. Make a total of 5 blocks.

2 When all of the blocks are pieced, press the blocks.

3 Square each block to 6½" × 8½" with the foundation side up (Crooked Cabins 1).

Applying Lattice to the Blocks

1 Sew a 1¼" × 8½" lattice strip to the right-hand side of each block. Press the seam allowances toward the lattice (Crooked Cabins 2).

2 Sew a 1¼" × 8½" lattice strip to the left-hand side of each block and press the seam allowances toward the lattice (Crooked Cabins 3).

3 Sew a cornerstone square on the ends of each 1¼" × 6½" lattice strip. Press the seam allowances toward the lattice.

4 Sew a strip from step 3 to the top of each cabin block. Press the seam allowances toward the lattice.

5 Arrange the cabin blocks in a vertical row. When you are pleased with the arrangement, sew the remaining strip from step 3 to the bottom of the bottom cabin block. Press the seam allowances toward the lattice.

6 Sew the blocks together in the vertical row to finish the quilt center. Press the seam allowances toward the lattice.

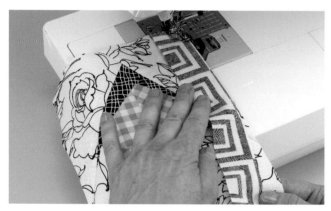

Crooked Cabins 2

Crooked Cabins 3

Crooked Cabins 4

Adding the Borders

1 Trim selvages off of the border strips and sew them together end to end into one long strip. Press the seams open.

2 From the long strip in step 1, cut 2 strips 4" × 45". Sew 1 strip to each side of the quilt center, and press the seams out.

3 From the remaining strip from step 1, cut 2 strips 4" × 15". Sew 1 strip each to the top and bottom of the quilt, and press the seams out.

Layering, Quilting, and Binding

1 Make a continuous 2¼" bias binding. Set aside.

2 Layer and quilt as desired. I quilted in a spiral out from the peepholes to invite any wandering birds to move in.

3 Bind and sign the quilt. Now you can hang up your cabins and wait for the flocks to arrive!

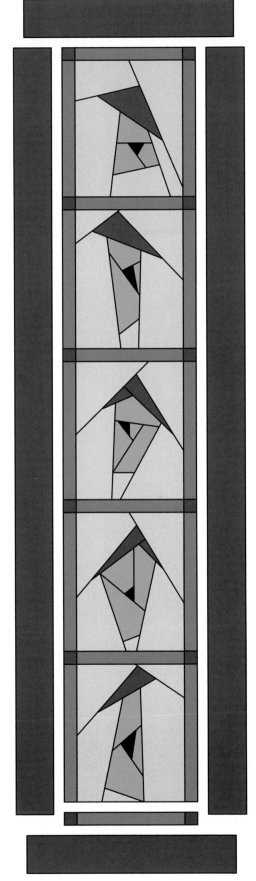

Crooked Cabins 5

Since my studio is in the basement of my home, I don't often take my machine away from its spot or sew away from home. However, I have had the fantastic opportunity to create while visiting my parents' summer home on Lake Wisconsin. I set up the sewing machine on the table on the porch. This is a typical Wisconsin porch, with windows on three sides and a beautiful lake right in front. That's what I call inspirational! On one of these trips, I was working on some sparse-looking trees. I had found an amazing vintage print that would become the border and a few contemporary pieces to complement it. The fabrics were sublime, the setting was unbeatable, and my children were happily playing on the beach right in front of me. This had to be foundation-piecing bliss! I was contentedly work-

ing along and decided to show my trees to my dad. Because their creation was taking place surrounded by Wisconsin beauty and because my dad had instilled in me a love of evergreens and a desire to save every seedling that crossed our paths, I was certain he would be as moved by this design as I was.

I proudly held up my trees for his approval. He proclaimed, "Those aren't trees. Those are electric poles." He could be right. He usually is. Yet, still I love my trees!

Pole Pines
Finished Quilt: 31½" × 40½"
Pieced and quilted by the author

materials

Background Fabric: 1½ yards

Pole Fabric: ⅓ yard

Pine Fabric: ⅝ yard

Lattice Fabric: ½ yard

Cornerstone Fabric: ⅛ yard

Border Fabric: ¾ yard

Binding: ⅝ yard

Backing: 1½ yards

Foundation Fabric: 3 yards of 12" wide foundation

Sulky Iron-On Transfer Pen

Batting: 39½" × 48½"

Fabric Suggestions

Let yourself go: Grab a vintage print that is a bit wild and wacky,

and build your trees to suit the border.

Mix contemporary prints with the vintage print for an

eclectic and funky quilt. Be brave and play!

cutting list

Strips are cut across the width of the fabric unless otherwise stated.

From Background Fabric, for Jack Pine (makes 2 blocks):
   Cut 1 strip 5½"
   Cut 1 strip 2½"
   Cut 1 strip 2"

From Background Fabric, for Red Pine (makes 2 blocks):
   Cut 1 strip 6½"
   Cut 1 strip 4"
   Cut 1 strip 3"
   Cut 1 strip 2"

From Background Fabric, for Norway Pine (makes 2 blocks):
   Cut 1 strip 5"
   Cut 1 strips 3½"
   Cut 1 strip 1½"

From Background Fabric, for White Pine (makes 3 blocks):
   Cut 1 strip 6½"
   Cut 2 strips 3"
   Cut 1 strip 2"

From Pine Fabric:
   Cut 7 strips 2¾"

From Pole Fabric:
   Cut 3 strips 3"

From Lattice Fabric:
   Cut 6 strips 1¼", then from these strips, cut the following
      12 strips 1¼" × 10½"
      12 strips 1¼" × 7½"

From Cornerstone Fabric:
   Cut 1 strip 1¼", then from this strip, cut the following
      16 squares 1¼" × 1¼"

From Border Fabric:
   Cut 4 strips 4", then from these strips, cut the following:
      2 strips 4" × 33½"
      2 strips 4" x 31½"

From Binding Fabric:
   Cut 1 square 20" × 20" to make 2¼" continuous bias binding

From Foundation Fabric:
   Cut 2 strips 11", then from these strips, cut the following:
      4 strips 11" × 8"

Pole Pines 1

Pole Pines 2

Pole Pines 3

Pole Pines 4

Preparation

1 With the iron-on transfer pen, trace each of the 4 *Pole Pine* patterns onto the foundation fabric. You will have two pieces for each pine. Mark a dot on the inner corners that will be matched when joining the sides of the trees together. Heat transfer each tree to an additional foundation piece. Select 1 tree to transfer a third time, for a total of 9 trees.

Piecing the Pole Pines

1 Foundation piece the Jack Pine half blocks according to the key and the numerical sequence on the foundation pattern. Use 5½", 2½", and 2" background strips. Press each half block, and trim on the inner cutting line where the halves will be joined. Set aside these half blocks (Pole Pines 1).

2 Foundation piece the Red Pine half blocks using 6½", 4", 3" and 2" background strips. Press each half block, and trim on the inner cutting line where the halves will be joined. Set aside these half blocks.

3 Foundation piece the White Pine half blocks using 6½", 3" and 2" background strips. Press each half block, and trim on the inner cutting line where the halves will be joined. Set aside these half blocks.

4 Foundation piece the Norway Pine half blocks using 5", 3½" and 1½" background strips. Press each half block, and trim on the inner cutting line where the halves will be joined. Set aside these half blocks.

5 Using perpendicular pinning (Pole Pines 2), join the Jack Pine half blocks to create complete blocks. Join all the half blocks in this fashion (Pole Pines 3), and press each seam whatever way it desires! No need to fight it—let it be happy. You will make a total of 9 blocks.

6 Square each block to 7½" × 10½" with the foundation up. Watch the pine points; be careful not to chop any off. These branches are far too young to be trimmed.

Applying Lattice to the Pines

1 Sew a 1¼" × 10½" lattice piece to the right-hand side of each block (Pole Pines 4). Press the seam allowances toward the lattice.

2 Arrange the blocks on a design wall, bed or clean floor in a 3 block × 3 block arrangement.

3 Sew a 1¼" × 10½" lattice piece to the left side of the left-most block in each row.

4 Sew the blocks in to three rows together. Press the seam allowances toward the lattice.

Joining the Rows with Lattice Strips

1 Gather 4 sets each consisting of 4 of the cornerstone squares (A) and 3 of the 7½" × 1¼" lattice strips (B).

2 Sew each set together in this order: A-B-A-B-A-B-A (Pole Pines 5). Press the seam allowances toward the lattice strips.

3 Sew 1 lattice set to the top of each row of pines (Pole Pines 6).

4 Sew 1 lattice strip set to the bottom of the bottom row of pines. Press the seam allowances toward the lattice sets (Pole Pines 7).

5 Join the rows and press seam allowances toward the lattice strip sets.

Adding the Border

1 Stitch a 4" × 33½" border strip to each side of the quilt center. Press the seams out.

2 Stitch a 4" × 31½" border strip to both the top and bottom of the quilt center. Press the seams out.

Layering, Quilting, and Binding

1 Infuse as much or as little energy as you want into this piece with the quilting. Perhaps you want to emphasize the sharp angles. In that case, quilt zigzags in the border and trees. Or soften the edges with a licorice whip.

2 To give it a more "grown-up" look, you could do some fancy swirls in the background as a delightful counterpoint to the branches. Whatever you decide, remember to sign your work (Pole Pines 8). Be proud of your accomplishments, and enjoy your Pole Pines or Electric Poles. Whatever you see is what they are!

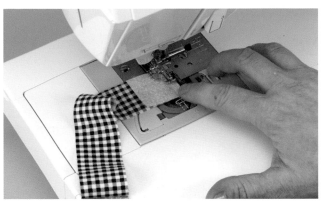

Pole Pines 5

Pole Pines 6

Pole Pines 7

Pole Pines 8

Hello, Heliconia!

The following is a cautionary tale. Forgotten quilt blocks remember you even if you forget about them. I had started a quilt with twelve floral blocks, and quite a bit of time elapsed from the start of that project to the end. A while after quilting and binding my *Garden Goddesses* quilt, I came across a block I had made for that quilt. It was a strikingly simple Heliconia flower. Obviously it never made it into the quilt. My remorse was so great that I quickly quilted and bound the fused design. I thought that would appease my regret (and the Heliconia), but it was not to be.

Soon after, I received a package of stunning flannel batiks from Bali Fabrics. The intense red tone-on-tone flannel was mesmerizing. Sometime during my fitful sleep that night, the red Bali flannel took it upon itself to become the perfect explosive touch to the uncomplicated design of the Heliconia. The clean, crisp angles of the exquisite Heliconia merged with the red Bali flannel to celebrate simple yet sharp beauty that is uncluttered and pure.

Early the next morning, the persistent flannel and the neglected flower woke me up and didn't let me rest until it had bloomed in fabric. No alarm clock is needed when you have captivating fabric and an "out of sight, out of mind" quilt block. Consider yourself warned.

Hello, Heliconia!

Finished Quilt: 21½" × 38½"
Pieced and quilted by the author
Fabrics courtesy of Bali Fabrics

materials

Black Geometric Print: ⅛ yard

Red Tone-on-Tone Flannel: ⅛ yard

Black With White Fern Print: ⅓ yard

Black Solid: 1 yard

Black With White String Print: ½ yard

Foundation Fabric: 1 yard of 12" wide foundation

Backing: ¾ yard

Batting: 29½" × 46½"

Sulky Iron-On Transfer Pen

Fabric Suggestions

Choose an incredible red flannel for the blossom.

The black prints should be of vastly different print styles.

This creates the chunky canvas for the Heliconia to stretch on.

Rich solid black is so important to this piece. Find one that

is deep and intense.

cutting list

Strips are cut across the width of the fabric unless otherwise stated.

From Black Solid (Border, Piecing, Foundation Piecing and Binding):
    Cut 1 strip 6"
    Cut 1 strip 3"
    Cut 3 strips 3½", then from these strips cut the following:
        3 rectangles 3½" × 10"
        1 rectangle 3½" × 21½"
        1 rectangle 3½" × 35"
    Cut 4 strips 2¼"

From Red Flannel (Piecing and Foundation Piecing):
    Cut 2 strips 1½"
    Cut 1 strip 1", then from this strip cut the following:
        1 rectangle 1" × 10"

From Black With White Fern Print (Foundation Piecing):
    Cut 1 strip 6½"
    Cut 1 strip 3"

From Black Geometric Print (Piecing):
    Cut 1 strip 3 ½", then from this strip cut the following:
        3 rectangles 3 ½" × 10"

From Black With White String Print (Border):
    Cut 3 strips 3½", then from these strips cut the following:
        2 rectangles 3½" × 35"
        2 rectangles 3½" × 12½"

From Foundation Fabric:
    Cut 3 squares 12" × 12"

Hello, Heliconia! 1

Hello, Heliconia! 2

Hello, Heliconia! 3

Hello, Heliconia! 4

Making the Blocks

1 Trace 3 copies of each half of the foundation pattern on foundation fabric.

2 Foundation piece each half block according to the number sequence and fabric key on the foundation pattern. Start with the left block section and use the solid black for the background. Press seams open with a wooden iron (Hello, Heliconia! 1).

3 Stitch the right block section in the same manner as the left section, only this time use the fern fabric instead of the solid black fabric. Press each half block, and trim evenly on the dashed (cutting) line. Sew the right and left block sections together along the middle stitching line using perpendicular pinning (Hello, Heliconia! 2). Press the seam open.

4 Repeat steps 2 and 3 to make a total of 3 blocks 6½" × 10".

Making the Rows

1 Join 1 black 3½" × 10" rectangle to 1 geometric 3½" × 10" rectangle. Press the seam allowance toward the black solid piece. Repeat to make a second set (Hello, Heliconia! 3).

2 Put aside one set from step 1 for Row 3. Join the other set from step 1 to the right-hand side of a Heliconia block, with the black strip adjoining the block (Hello, Heliconia! 4). Press the seam toward the black piece. This is Row 1.

3 Add 1 geometric print 3½" × 10" rectangle to the left-hand side of a Heliconia block. Add 1 solid black 3½" × 10" rectangle to the right-hand side of the same Heliconia block (Hello, Heliconia! 5). Press seams toward the solid black. This is Row 2.

4 Add the set of a solid black rectangle with a geometric rectangle (the one you set aside in step 2) to the left side of the remaining Heliconia block (Hello, Heliconia! 6). Press the seam toward the black fabric. This is Row 3.

5 Fold the 1" × 10" red flannel rectangle in half lengthwise with wrong sides together and press. Stitch the folded strip to the left side of Row 3 with a ⅛" seam (Hello, Heliconia! 7). It will be a folded tweaker border that remains flat over the block, toward the row.

6 Sew the rows together, matching all seams, to assemble the 12½" × 29" quilt center, and press.

Adding the Borders:

1 Stitch a 3½" × 12½" black string print rectangle to the top and another to the bottom of the quilt center. Press the seams out.

2 Stitch a 3½" × 35" black string print rectangle to each side of the quilt center, and press the seams out.

3 Stitch a 3½" × 35" solid black rectangle to the left side of the quilt center. Press the seam out.

4 Stitch a 3½" × 21½" solid black rectangle to the bottom of the quilt center, and press the seam out. You did it! It is time to layer, quilt, and bind! Once again my laziness shines through. I have chosen fabulous fabrics that don't require a lot of quilting to create a beautiful quilt. Simple vertical lines with nothing on the flowers does the trick!

Hello, Heliconia! 5

Hello, Heliconia! 6

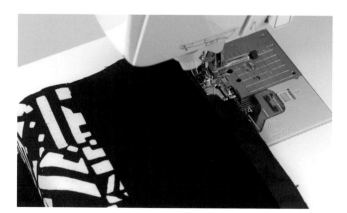

Hello, Heliconia! 7

Ah, silk. This quilt was born out of my desire to play with luscious, gorgeous and vibrant silk. I find tall evergreens quite refined and stately, so naturally I gravitated toward creating a tree with silk. My designs are typically spare and angular. That description doesn't automatically lead to silk. However, if you focus on the fabric as the star of the design and the tree as only its vessel, the choice of silk makes a lot more sense. Simple tree, simply beautiful fabric.

Royaltry

Finished Quilt: 39" × 47"

Pieced and quilted by the author

materials list

Background and Pieced Border: 1⅜ yards of solid white silk

Tree and Pieced Border: ⅝ yard solid green silk

Borders and Binding: 1¾ yards solid black silk

Backing: 2¾ yards white cotton

Batting: 47" × 55"

Foundation Fabric: 3¼ yards of 12" wide

Fabric Suggestions

Try using some luscious fabric that you have shied away from in the past. I'll hold your hand.

Choose rich, deep color since there are very few fabrics and they need to be bold and captivating all on their own.

I used silk; perhaps you'll try flannel or velvet or even "unknown fabric content"! I dare you!

cutting list

Strips are cut across the width of the fabric unless otherwise stated.

From White Solid:
Cut 1 strip 9½"
Cut 4 strips 5½"
Cut 3 strips 4"

From Green Solid:
Cut 2 strips 4"
Cut 3 strips 2½"
Cut 1 strip 1½"

From Black Solid (Inner Border, Outer Border):
Cut 4 strips 2¼", then from these strips cut the following:
2 strips 2¼" × 30½"
2 strips 2¼" × 26"
Cut 4 strips 5½", then from these strips cut the following:
2 strips 5½" × 38"
2 strips 5½" × 40"

From Binding:
Cut 1 square 20" × 20" to make 2¼" continuous binding

From Foundation Fabric:
Cut 2 strips 12" × 32"
Cut 4 strips 3" × 40"

Silk Tips

If you choose to use silk for your tree, here are some tips:

- *Turn your iron down!*

- *Be diligent in finding the grain line when you cut your border strips. This will help reduce unraveling.*

- *If you are at all like me, you will be tempted to pull on those "ravely" threads—don't! Cut all stragglers.*

- *Use a ⅜" seam allowance.*

- *Don't get discouraged by the shifting and rippling of the silk; consider it added texture and delight in the shimmer of the silk!*

- *Enjoy the wonderful sound of the needle popping through the silk. It is not the "swoosh" of cotton, and it startled me at first!*

- *Trim your seam allowances carefully. Do not let any dark fabric extend past your light silk; it will show through to the front of your quilt. Take the time to trim twice, trimming the dark layer a smidge narrower than the light layer.*

- *After your final pressing, check again for any unraveling so you don't end up with dark strays showing through the light-colored silk.*

- *Serge or staystitch around the outer edges of the finished quilt top. That will help reduce ravels.*

Enjoy searching for wonderful silks. Try your local quilt shop, online shops and other fabric shops, or scour estate sales or even your mother's closet. I have my mom's old silk robe ready to chop up and piece—nothing is safe!

Preparation

1 Enlarge the foundation patterns by 400 percent. Trace 1 copy of each enlarged half onto one of the 12" × 32" foundation strips.

Piecing the Tree

1 Foundation piece each tree half according to numerical sequence and strip width on the foundation pattern.

2 Press each section, and trim on the cutting lines. Save the scraps to use for the pieced border.

3 Using perpendicular pinning, stitch the 2 tree halves together to make the tree.

4 Press the seam allowance toward the tree trunk. The tree block should measure 22½" × 30½".

Royaltry 1

Piecing the Foundation Borders

1 Foundation piece the 3" × 40" border strips using triangles of white and green fabric scraps and the remaining black fabric (Royaltry 1).

2 Press the strips. Trim 2 strips to 2½" × 34" strips and 2 strips to 2½" × 30".

Adding the Borders

1 Sew a 2¼" × 30½" black inner border strip to each side of the tree block. Press the seam allowances out toward the borders.

2 Sew a 2¼" × 26" black inner border strip to the top and to the bottom of the tree block. Press the seams out toward the border.

3 Sew a 2½" × 34" pieced border strips to each side of the quilt. Press the seams in toward the inner border.

4 Sew a 2½" × 30" pieced inner border strip to the top and to the bottom of the quilt center. Press the seams in toward the foundation border.

5 Sew a 5½" × 38" outer border strip to each side of the quilt center. Press the seams out toward the border.

6 Sew a 5½" × 40" outer border strip to the top and to the bottom of the quilt center. Press the seams out toward the border.

Royaltry 2

Layering, Quilting, and Binding

1 Layer, quilt and bind your creation.

2 Take pride in your work by signing and dating the quilt or attaching a personalized label to it.

Royaltry 3

Cocktails With Val

Val has a date. For quite some time she has been successfully ignoring the gorgeous guy in 3B, thinking all along that a career and her cats are fine substitutes for cocktails and dinner. Her momentary lapse in judgment has put her in the position not only of opening her mind to something other than work but of getting ready to do it in thirty minutes! Resigned to her fate, she opens her closet door to select a cocktail dress. She never realized she had so many little black dresses to choose from! Seeking help from her feline companions, she shows them dress after dress in hopes of an affirmative reaction. Down to fifteen minutes and counting, she resorts to closing her eyes and grabbing.

Val is not one to do anything halfheartedly. Not only is she throwing caution to the wind and "seizing the day," she is seizing the dress as well!

Cocktails With Val

Finished Quilt: 42½" × 19½"
Pieced and quilted by the author

materials

Background Fabric: ½ yard

Dress Fabric: 3 fat quarters

Martini Glass Fabric: ⅛ yard

Liquid in Glass Fabric: ⅛ yard

Lattice Fabric: ¼ yard

Zinger Cornerstone Fabric: ⅛ yard

Border Fabric: ⅝ yard

Snazzy Binding Fabric: ½ yard (18" square)

Backing: 1¼ yards

Batting size: 50" × 28"

Embellishments: olives, pimentos, swizzle sticks, and froufrou for the dresses—have fun!

Foundation Fabric: 2 yards of 12" wide foundation

Sulky Iron-On Transfer pen

1 sheet of paper 8 ½ " × 11"

Pen or pencil

Fabric Suggestions

The sky is the limit here! Throw all of those fun girly prints together to make a charming quilt.

Do make sure that there is enough contrast between the dresses and background.

Make your zinger clear and strong. This zinger needs to sing out from the corners of the quilt and set the mood. Red is a classic choice.

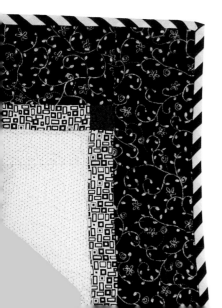

cutting list

Strips are cut across the width of the fabric unless otherwise stated.

From Cornerstone Fabric:
    Cut 1 strip 1½", then from these strips cut the following:
        10 squares 1½" × 1½"

From Lattice Fabric:
    Cut 4 strips 1½", then from these strips cut the following:
        5 strips 1½" × 10½"
        8 strips 1½" × 8"

From Border Fabric:
    Cut 4 strips 4", then from these strips cut the following:
        2 strips 4" × 35½"
        2 strips 4" × 19½"

From Foundation Fabric:
    Cut 3 squares 12" x 12" for dresses
    1 rectangle 12" x 18" for martini

From Binding Fabric:
    Cut 1 square 18" x 18" to make 2¼" continuous bias binding

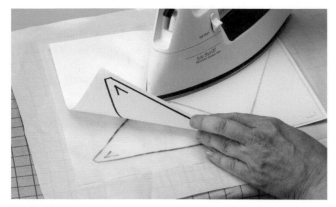

Cocktails With Val 1

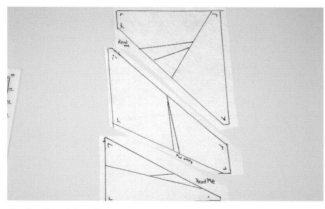

Cocktails With Val 2

Cocktails With Val 3

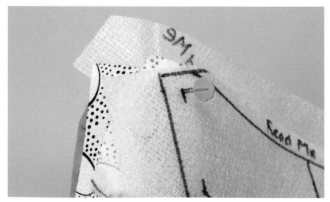

Cocktails With Val 4

Preparation

1 With the transfer pen, trace the 2 sections (bodice and skirt) of Val's dress onto a sheet of white 8½" × 11" paper. Put dots in the corners of the seams that will be joined; this will aid in piecing later on. Heat-transfer 3 copies of each half onto the 12" x 12" foundation fabric (Cocktails With Val 1).

2 With a pen or pencil, trace the 3 sections of the martini glass onto sheets of 12" x 18" foundation fabric. Mark the corners of the seams with dots to aid with perpendicular pinning.

Piecing the Blocks

1 Foundation piece the dress halves according to the fabric key and numerical sequence on the foundation pattern (Cocktails With Val 2). Use each fat quarter to piece 1 dress. Maintain the same fabric within each block.

2 Press each dress half. Trim on the cutting line on the joint of the dress sections.

3 To make the first dress, perpendicularly pin through the corresponding dots in the upper and lower corners of the dress sections and sew the seam. Press the seam open. Repeat to make the other 2 dresses.

4 Foundation piece the 3 sections of the martini block. The martini glass may seem confusing, like a bunch of crazy triangles, until you line them up. Then you can see the martini glass (Cocktails With Val 3).

5 Press each section of the martini block. Trim ¼" past the seam lines to be joined.

6 Perpendicularly pin through the corresponding dots and arrows to align the sections of the martini glass (Cocktails With Val 4), and sew the seams. Press the seams open.

7 Trim each dress block and the martini block to 8" × 10½" with the foundation side up.

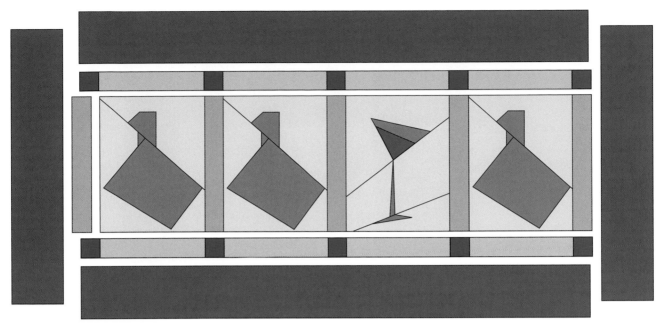

Cocktails With Val 5

Putting the Blocks in Rows

1 Sew a 1½" × 10½" lattice strip to the right-hand side of each dress block and the martini block. Press the seam allowances toward the lattice.

2 On a design wall, bed or clean floor, arrange the blocks according to the quilt layout diagram.

3 Sew the blocks together to form 1 row of 4 blocks. Press the seams toward the lattice.

4 Sew a 1½" × 10½" lattice strip to the left side of the left-most block in the row. Press the seam toward the lattice.

Adding Lattice

1 Gather 2 sets each consisting of 3 cornerstone squares (A) and 2 of the lattice strip (B). Sew together 1 set in this combination: A-B-A-B-A-B-A-B-A. Repeat for the other set. Press the seams toward the lattice strips.

2 Sew 1 lattice strip from step 1 to the top of the row of blocks. Sew the other strip from step 1 to the bottom row.

3 Press the seams toward the lattice.

Adding Borders

1 Sew a 4" × 35½" border to the top and to the bottom of the quilt center. Press the seams out toward the border.

2 Sew a 4" × 19½" border to each side of the quilt center. Press the seams allowances out toward the borders.

Layering, Accessorizing, Quilting, Binding

1 Make 2¼" continuous bias binding from the snazzy fabric.

2 It is completely up to you whether you add froufrou now or later or not at all. After binding the quilt, you could still stitch or glue on additional gems, flowers, beads, or sequins.

3 I added ribbons, bows, fringe and other assorted embellishments.

4 I used a vintage button and yarn to make the swizzle stick and the olive in the martini.

5 Make sure to sign and date the quilt or attach a personalized label to it.

Elegance

This quilt presented a challenge for me. I don't often use fabric from the same line or even the same manufacturer to complete a quilt top because I look for more contrast and scale differences than one line typically offers. This line was an exception. It offered everything I needed to create *Elegance*.

The fabrics led me to the design, not the other way around. The subtle scale differences urged me to play with movement, depth and flow instead of thinking in terms of a finite quilt block. As soon as I let the fabrics frolic for awhile, they fell into place as an Oriental fan resting on a fluid yet structured canvas. The surprising fuchsia zinger adds the necessary sass to an otherwise elegant creation.

I encourage all of my students to be free and forget about the quilting police, yet I have a few set rules for myself. I may not consciously adhere to them, but they exist nonetheless. It's good for me to break some of my rules at times. Experiments like this often lead me to unexpected and delightful conclusions that I would miss if I didn't step out of my box now and again. If I remember to step back, take my time, and let the fabric play, amazing things happen!

Elegance
Finished Quilt: 36" × 47"
Pieced and quilted by the author
Fabrics courtesy of Maywood Fabrics

materials

Fan Fabric: ¼ yard of 5 different dark black with white prints (label them a, b, c, d, and e)

Fan Background and Lattice Fabric: ⅞ yard large-scale white with black print

Cornerstone Background Fabric: ¼ yard medium-scale white with black print

Inner Border Fabric: ½ yard large-scale very light white with black print

Outer Border Fabric: ⅔ yard large-scale dark black with white print

Cornerstone Color and Zinger Border Fabric: ¼ yard zippy pink

Binding Fabric: ⅔ yard medium-scale medium black with white print

Foundation Fabric: 4½ yards of 12" wide foundation

Backing: 1½ yards light large-scale white with black print

Batting: crib size

Sulky Iron-On Transfer Pen

Several pieces of white 8½" × 11" paper

cutting list

Strips are cut across the width of the fabric unless otherwise stated.

From Fan Fabric:
 Cut 3 strips 2¼" from fabrics a, b, c and d
 Cut 2 strips 2¼" from fabric e

From Fan Background and Lattice Fabric:
 Cut 2 strips 3"
 Cut 7 strips 2½", then from these strips cut the following:
  17 strips 2½" × 9½"

From Cornerstone Background Fabric:
 Cut 3 strips 2"

From Cornerstone Color and Zinger Border Fabric:
 Cut 5 strips 1¼", then from these strips cut the following:
  2 strips 1¼" × 40½"
  2 strips 1¼" × 29½"
  12 strips 1¼" × 1¼"

From Inner Border Fabric:
 Cut 4 strips 3", then from these strips cut the following:
  2 strips 3" × 40½"
  2 strips 3" × 24½"

From Outer Border Fabric:
 Cut 4 strips 4", then from these strips cut the following:
  2 strips 4" × 36½"
  2 strips 4" × 40½"

From Binding Fabric:
 Cut 1 square 20" × 20" to make 2¼" continuous bias binding

From Foundation Fabric:
 Cut 6 squares 12" × 12"
 Cut 12 squares 3" × 3"

Fabric Suggestions

Try to sneak a bit of fun into this elegant piece. The fuchsia cornerstones add gaiety and spunk.

Practice evaluating scale, and audition many pieces to get your fan just right. Can you see it unfold? If you can, the fabrics are just right!

The background and lattice fabrics have just a slight variation in value. This creates a subtle shift in the quilt instead of a strong delineation. It would be great to see this piece done in a completely different manner. What about a tropical theme? Or perhaps using fabrics with a greater value difference for the lattice and background? Or purple in the corner? Set your creativity free!

Play with backgrounds that step gently from one scale to another. How smooth can you make that transition with three different fabrics?

The fans include a variety of black prints close in value but varying in scale. They are closer together in value than fabrics I typically choose, but this tight palette adds to the graceful look of the piece.

The cornerstone color needs to be strong enough to catch your eye yet not strong enough to dominate the fans.

The outer and inner borders can repeat fabrics used in the fans or bring in different fabrics. I enjoy introducing new fabrics in the border. In a class somewhere along the line I was discouraged from doing that, which must be why I embrace the practice! I have had difficulty coloring inside the lines and following the quilting "rules"!

Preparation

1 Using an iron-on transfer pen, trace 1 copy of each section of the fan and cornerstone patterns onto a piece of white paper.

2 Iron the fan patterns directly to each of the 6 foundation fabric 12" × 12" squares.

3 Iron the cornerstone patterns directly to each of the 12 foundation fabric 3" × 3" squares.

4 If the ink becomes too faint, retrace the existing lines on the paper with the iron-on pen and keep going!

Piecing the Sections

1 Foundation piece the big fan sections in numerical order using the letters printed on the foundation pattern for fabric placement.

2 Foundation piece the smaller fan sections in numerical order using the letter for fabric placement. Note that e is the only fabric that does not repeat.

3 Press the half blocks, and trim only on the inner cutting lines (Elegance 1)

4 Using perpendicular pinning, join the 2 fan sections and, press the seam open.

5 Square the fans blocks to 9½" × 9½" (Elegance 2).

6 Foundation piece the cornerstone blocks to make wonky squares in a square look (Elegance 3). Press the blocks, and square them to 2½" × 2½"

Elegance 1

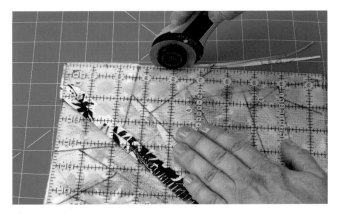

Elegance 2

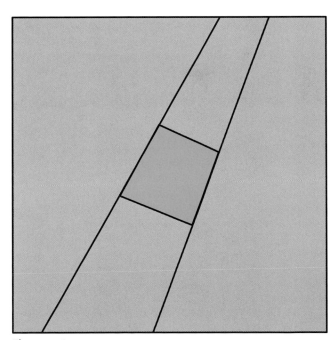

Elegance 3

Elegance 4

Assembling the Rows

1 Sew a 2½" × 9½" lattice strip to the right-hand side of each fan block. Press the seam allowances toward the lattice.

2 Join 2 fan blocks with lattice in between to make a row. Repeat to make a total of three rows. Press the seams toward the lattice.

3 Sew a lattice strip to the left side of each row. Press the seam allowances toward the lattice.

Joining the Rows With Lattice

1 Gather 4 sets each consisting of 3 cornerstone blocks (Y) and 2 of the 2" x 8" strips (Z). Sew together 1 set in this pattern: Y-Z-Y-Z-Y. Repeat for the other 3 sets (Elegance 6).

2 Press the seams toward the lattice.

3 Sew 1 lattice strip from step 1 to the top of each row of blocks. Press the seams toward the lattice.

4 Sew 1 lattice strip to the bottom of one row. This is the bottom row. Press the seam toward the lattice.

5 Join the 3 rows of fans to complete the quilt center. Press the seam allowances toward the lattice.

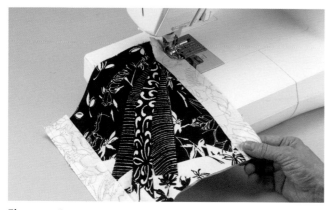

Elegance 5

Elegance 6

Adding the Borders

1 Sew 1 of the 3" × 24½" strips to the top and to the bottom of the quilt center. Press the seams out toward the border.

2 Sew a 3" × 40½" inner border strip to each side of the quilt center. Press the seams out toward the border.

3 Fold and press each zinger border strip in half lengthwise, wrong sides together (Elegance 7) .

4 Line up the raw edge of 1 of the 1¼" × 29½" zinger border strips to the top of the quilt center and then sew to the quilt center with a ⅛" seam. Repeat at the bottom of the quilt center with the other 1¼" × 29½" zinger border strip.

5 Line up the raw edges and sew a 1¼" × 40½" zinger border strip to each side of the quilt center with a ⅛" seam. Do not press these borders out.

6 Sew a 4" × 40½" outer border strip to each side of the quilt center, sandwiching the zinger border (Elegance 8).

7 Sew 1 of the 4" × 36½" outer border strips to the top of the quilt center and 1 to the bottom, sandwiching the zinger border.

8 Press the seams out toward the border, keeping the zinger borders pointing in toward the quilt center (Elegance 9).

Layering, Quilting and Binding

1 Layer, quilt and bind your creation. When using fabrics this busy, the quilting is going to show only as texture, unless you use contrasting thread. I like to stay out of the way of the fabric and let it do the work. I basically quilted the piece to hold it together and add some dimension, not to add design elements.

2 Take pride in your work by signing and dating the quilt or attaching a personalized label to it.

Elegance 7

Elegance 8

Elegance 9

Hurry Up, Spring!

There is nothing quite as magical as watching tender young plants break through the soil and stretch toward the sun. Quilted posies illustrate that story in this fabric tribute to the clay pot.

Stashed in just about every garage in the Western world, clay pots mother and nurture our indoor gardens as the tender shoots reach for the sky. Each row of this quilt represents a different stage of growth. Emergence, stretching and graceful reaching for the sun are quilted with colorful thread to entice a closer look. Are they growing, or aren't they?

Hurry Up, Spring!

Finished Quilt: 26" × 42"
Pieced and quilted by the author
Black-and-white batiks courtesy of Bali Fabrics

materials

Background Fabric: 1¼ yards light white-textured solid

Pot Fabric: ⅛ yard each of 6 prints of dark, white-on-black prints varying in scale

Inner Border and Lattice Fabric: ⅜ yard dark, white-on-black medium-scale print

Outer Border Fabric: 1 yard medium dark, white-on-black large-scale print

Cornerstone Fabric: ⅛ yard vibrant orange

Binding Fabric: ⅝ yard dark black print

Foundation Fabric: 5 yards of 8" wide foundation

Backing: 1½ yards light, white-on-white

Batting: 34" × 50"

Sulky Iron-On Transfer Pen

Several pieces of 8½" × 11" white paper

cutting list

Strips are cut across the width of the fabric unless otherwise stated.

From Background Fabric:
 Cut 1 strip 7½"
 Cut 1 strip 6¾"
 Cut 2 strips 3½"
 Cut 3 strips 2"
 Cut 4 strips 1½"

From Pot Fabric:
 Cut 1 strip 3" from each of the 6 fabrics

From Inner Border and Lattice Fabric:
 Cut 2 strips 2", then from these strips, cut the following:
  1 strip 2" × 23¾"
  3 strips 2" × 9½"
 Cut 2 strips 3", then from these strips, cut the following:
  1 strip 3" × 23¾"
  3 strips 3" × 9½"
 Cut 2 strips 1½", then from these strips, cut the following:
  2 strips 1½" × 23¾" for lattice

From Outer Border Fabric:
 Cut 2 strips 3½", then from these strips, cut the following:
  1 strip 3½" × 26¼" (top)
  1 strip 3½" × 33½" (right)
 Cut 2 strips 5" then from these strips, cut the following:
  1 strip 5" × 33½" (left)
  1 strip 5" × 33¾" (bottom)

From Cornerstone Fabric:
 Cut 1 strip 3", then from these strips, cut the following:
  1 square 3" × 3"
  1 strip 3" × 2"
  2 strips 3" × 1½"

From Binding Fabric:
 Cut 1 square 20" × 20" to make 2¼" continuous bias binding

From Foundation Fabric:
 Cut 18 rectangles 8" x 10"

My Fabric Selections

I used a vintage bark cloth type fabric for the background. The texture provides interest in the repeating expanses of background.

Since all of the prints are filled with movement, I chose one of the darkest prints to anchor the quilt in the inner border (left). The large scale of the outer border (right) balances the activity of the quilt center.

Smooth Bali batiks contrast the nubby background. I enjoy mixing the modern and old for surprising texture combinations and effects.

The deep orange/pink/red batik adds richness and punch.

Preparation

1 Using an iron-on transfer pen, trace one copy of each pot pattern onto a piece of white paper.

2 Heat-transfer the patterns directly on the 8" x 10" foundation rectangles. Continue transferring until you have 3 copies of each pot.

3 For this design, you may mark the numbers in the pots to aid in piecing. Since I leave the foundation in the quilt, I don't mark the numbers on the background sections. Otherwise the numbers may show through the background.

4 Separate the pots, and make 1 stack of each type of pot. Lay the 6 stacks as they will appear in the quilt and designate them from A to F.

Piecing the Pots

1 Foundation piece 1 Pot A. Repeat for the second and third Pot A, using a different fabric for each pot. Finger press the pots, and trim each seam allowance as you go. Restack this pot set.

2 Repeat step 1 for Pot B, Pot C, Pot D, Pot E and Pot F.

3 Use an iron to press each pot. Trim carefully on the cutting lines.

Assembling the Pots

1 Lay out the pots in 3 rows so that each row has 6 pots, in order from A to F (Hurry Up, Spring! 1).

2 Sew together Pots A and B from row 1 (Hurry Up, Spring! 2). Leave them in the sewing machine, and do not cut the thread. Chain stitch Pots A and B from row 2 , followed by Pots A and B from row 3. Again, do not cut the thread.

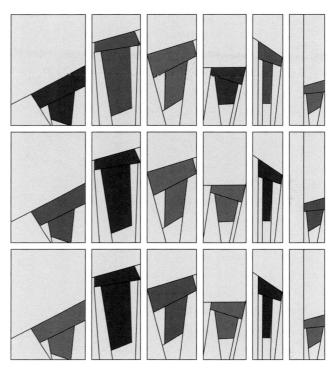

Hurry Up, Spring! 1

Hurry Up, Spring! 2

3 Continue the chain with Pots C and D from each row (Hurry Up, Spring! 3).

4 Join Pots E and F in exactly the same manner (Hurry Up, Spring! 4). Do *not* touch that thread until all of the pots are joined in sets of two. Keeping the pots in "chains" mean they can't move out of place and get out of order.

5 Remove the "chain" of pots from the machine and locate the beginning of the chain. Count down three pairs of pots; this is the end of the Pot A and Pot B pairs. Snip the connecting threads between the last Pot A and Pot B pair and the first Pot C and Pot D pair.

6 Sew together each Pot B and Pot C set in order down the chain. This creates three rows of Pots A, B, C and D (Hurry Up, Spring! 5). Remove the 3 rows of 4 pots from the machine and clip the threads.

7 Repeat step 6 to attach the Pot E and Pot F pairs to each row, sewing each Pot E to the right of the Pot D from that row (Hurry Up, Spring! 6).

8 Remove the completed chain, clip the threads and press the seam allowances all toward the same side.

Hurry Up, Spring! 3

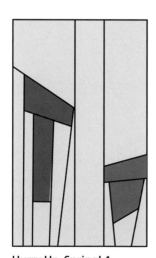

Hurry Up, Spring! 4

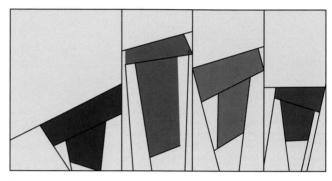

Hurry Up, Spring! 5

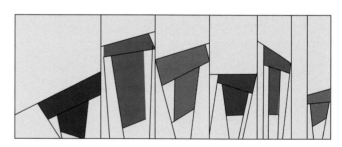

Hurry Up, Spring! 6

Adding Inner Borders and Lattice

1 Sew a 2" × 9½" inner border strip to the right-hand side of each row (Hurry Up, Spring! 7). Press the seam allowance toward the inner border.

2 Sew a 2" × 23¾" inner border strip to the top of Row 1 only (Hurry Up, Spring! 8). Press the seam allowance toward the inner border.

3 Sew a 3" × 23¾" inner border strip to the bottom Row 3 only (Hurry Up, Spring! 9). Press the seam allowance toward the inner border.

4 Sew a 1½" × 23¾" lattice strip to the bottom of Row 1 (Hurry Up, Spring! 10) and the bottom of Row 2. Press the seam allowances toward the lattice.

5 Sew Rows 1 and 2 together. Press the seam allowance toward the lattice.

6 Sew Row 3 to Row 2. Press seam allowance toward the lattice.

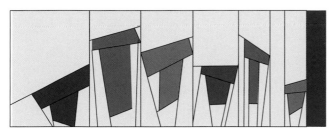

Hurry Up, Spring! 7

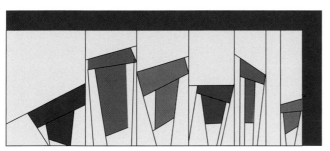

Hurry Up, Spring! 8

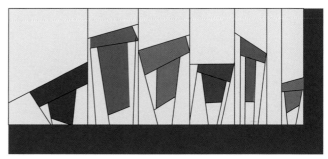

Hurry Up, Spring! 9

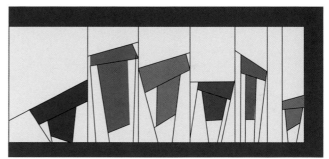

Hurry Up, Spring! 10

Adding the Color

1 Sew a 1½" × 3" cornerstone strip to each end of a 3" × 9½" inner border strip. This is the center section of the left inner border.

2 Sew a 3" × 2" cornerstone strip to the end of a 3" × 9½" inner border strip. This is the top section of the left inner border.

3 Sew together the sections from steps 1 and 2.

4 Sew the 3" × 3" cornerstone square to 1 end of the last 3" × 9½" inner border strip.

5 Join the inner border strip from step 4 to the section from step 3.

6 Press the seam allowances toward the inner border strips. The left inner border is now complete

7 Sew the left inner border strip to the left side of the quilt center, with the 3" × 3" cornerstone square at the bottom of the left inner border. Match the seams at the cornerstones.

Hurry Up, Spring 11

Adding the Outer Border

1 Sew the 3½" × 26¼" outer border strip to the top of the quilt center. Press the seam allowance out toward the border.

2 Sew the 3½" × 33½" outer border strip to the right-hand side of the quilt center. Press the seam allowance out toward the border.

3 Sew the 5" × 33½" outer border strip to the left side of the quilt center.. Press the seam allowance out toward the border.

4 Sew the 5"× 33¾" outer border strip to the bottom of the quilt center. Press the seam allowance out toward the border.

Layering, Binding, and Quilting

1 To show the growing progression of the flowers, quilt sprouts coming out of the pots in Row 2 and flowers coming out of the pots in Row 3.

2 Instead of quilting the plants, you can experiment and do a wide range of things. You might appliqué or embroider flowers by hand or machine. You could keep all the pots empty, as I have done in Row 1. Add flowers and then embellish them, or draw and color flowers onto the quilt. The only requirement is that you use your imagination and make your own personal statement.

3 The quilted leaves and flowers in this quilt are not visible until you get up close. I really enjoy adding surprises like that to my quilts. It is like having a secret that you get to tell!

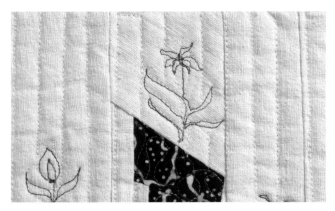

Hurry Up, Spring! 12

Hurry Up, Spring! 13

Fish Tales

In a dark world illuminated only by the pink fish that inhabit the depths, Bubblejoy frolics and plays in the knowledge that undulating values in and of themselves do not guarantee happiness. Salmon subtlety is beautiful and alluring. However, nuanced scales are not the only option. Giggling as she wiggles and romps, Bubble-joy proudly displays her bubbles against her pale pink skin. A delightful difference yields charming giggles. Bubbles and joy. Ahh!

Fish Tales

Finished Quilt: 78½" × 66½"
Pieced and quilted by the author

materials

Very dark, white-on-black large-scale sunburst print: 1 yard

Dark, white-on-black large-scale floral print: ⅝ yard

Medium dark, white-on-black large-scale floral outline print: 1¼ yards

Medium dark, white-on-black large-scale meteor drop print: ⅞ yard

Medium dark, white-on-black seagull print: 1¼ yards

Medium dark, white-on-black dash-dot print: ⅔ yard

Medium, white-on-black polka-dot print: ½ yard

Medium, white-on-black chopstick print: ½ yard

Rose-to-pink gradated fabric: ⅝ yard

Binding Fabric: ¾ yard

Backing: 4¼ yards

Several pieces of white paper 8½" x 11"

Sulky Iron-On Transfer Pen

Foundation: 4½ yards of 8" wide foundation

Fabric Suggestions

I used a variety of batiks from SewBatik. The black is very rich and dark. That is critical for me when I use batik.

The backgrounds for the fish can be a medium dark, but keep the pieced strips a darker value. If any strips have a lighter value, they will pull draw attention and diminish the impact of the design. We don't want to muddy the water!

Fabrics with gradation are fun to play with. Choose one you love or substitute four or five fabrics of slightly different values for a scrappier look.

cutting list

Strips are cut across the width of the fabric unless otherwise stated.

From Sunburst Print:
　Cut 5 strips 6½", then from these strips cut the following:
　　3 strips 6½" × 18½"
　　5 strips 6½" × 12½"
　　6 squares 6½" × 6½"
　　6 strips 6½" × 3½"

From Floral Print:
　Cut 1 strips 6½", then from this strip cut the following:
　　1 square 6½" × 6½"
　　3 strips 6½" × 3½"
　Cut 1 strip 4"
　Cut 3 strips 3"

From Floral Outline Print:
　Cut 4 strips 6½", then from these strips cut the following:
　　8 strips 6½" × 12½"
　　3 squares 6½" × 6½"
　　1 strip 6½" × 3½"
　Cut 2 strips 4"
　Cut 2 strips 2½"

From Meteor Drop Print:
　Cut 4 strips 6½", then from these strips cut the following:
　　3 strips 6½" × 18½"
　　6 strips 6½" × 12½"
　　2 squares 6½" × 6½"
　　3 strips 6½" × 3½"

From Seagull Print:
　Cut 6 strips 6½", then from these strips cut the following:
　　1 strip 6½" × 36½"
　　2 strips 6½" × 18½"
　　8 strips 6½" × 12½"
　　3 squares 6½" × 6½"
　　1 strip 6½" × 3½"

From Dash-Dot Print:
　Cut 3 strips 6½", then from these strips cut the following:
　　1 strip 6½" × 36½"
　　3 strips 6½"× 12½"
　　3 squares 6½" × 6½'

From Polka-Dot Print:
　Cut 2 strips 3½"
　Cut 2 strips 3"

From Chopstick Print:
　Cut 2 strips 3½"
　Cut 2 strips 2½"

From Gradated Fabric:
　Cut 7 strips 2½"

From Binding Fabric:
　Cut 1 square 28" × 28" to make 2¼" continuous bias binding

From Foundation Fabric:
　Cut 22 rectangles 7" x 8"

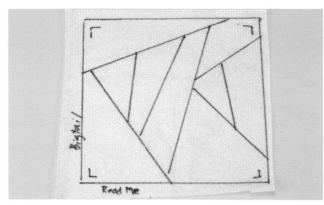

Fish Tales 1

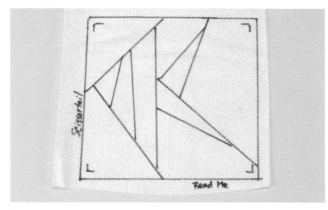

Fish Tales 2

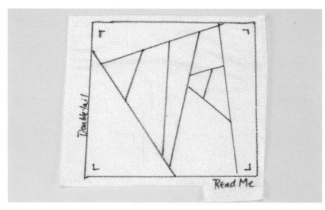

Fish Tales 3

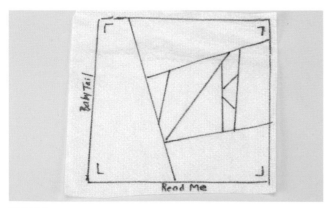

Fish Tales 4

Preparation

1 Trace each of the 4 fish foundations patterns onto 8½" × 11" white paper with an iron-on transfer pen.

2 Heat-transfer the designs onto your foundation fabric as follows: 5 copies of Doubletail, 6 copies or Scissortail, 5 copies of Bigtail, and 6 copies of Babytail.

3 Say "four fish foundations" 10 times fast. Smile.

Piecing the Fishies

1 Foundation piece all 5 Bigtail blocks with the strips of the floral outline fabric. Use the darkest end of a gradated strip for Section 1.

Section 2 is from the lightest end of the gradated strip. Piece the rest of Bigtail using the gradated strip from dark to light in succession.

2 Foundation piece all 6 Scissortail blocks with the strips of floral fabric. Use the lightest end of a gradated strip for the tail sections and move toward the darkest end for the nose sections.

3 Foundation piece all 5 Doubletail blocks with polka-dot fabric. Use the darkest end of a gradated strip on the tail sections, and move toward the lightest end for the nose sections.

4 Foundation piece all 6 Babytail blocks with the chopstick print. Start with the lightest end of a gradated strip for the tails, and work toward the darkest end for the noses. One of my Babytail blocks (which I named "Bubblejoy") has a barely perceptible gradation, leaving the Babytail almost all light. I flipped this block in my quilt top so he heads off in the other direction. Tailor your blocks to your sensibilities and preferences.

5 Press all the blocks and square them to 6½" × 6½". Be careful when squaring up the blocks. This is not a filleting step: We don't want any fins, noses or tails trimmed off.

Piecing the Vertical Rows

1 Place the strips and fish blocks onto the design wall as they appear in the quilt diagram.

2 Stitch the strips and fish blocks for 1 vertical row together. Repeat for each of the other 10 vertical rows.

3 Press the seams in the odd-numbered rows down and the seams in even-numbered rows up. This will allow the few seam that meet to interlock and lay as flat as possible.

4 Stitch Rows 1 and 2 together, and press the seam.

5 Stitch Rows 3 and 4 together, and press the seam. Continue joining 2 rows together. Row 11 will remain alone for now.

6 Stitch Rows 1-2 to Rows 3-4 and press.

7 Stitch Rows 5-6 to Rows 7-8 and press.

8 Stitch Rows 9-10 to Row 11 and press.

9 Join the three sections in order, and press the seams.

Fish Tales 6

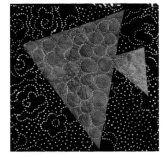
Fish Tales 7

Fish Tales 8

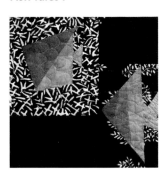
Fish Tales 9

Layering, Binding and Quilting

1 The fish scales are different by type of fish. This adds a bit of interest and varying texture. Bubblejoy's story dictated the quilting. This palest little fish in the upper-right corner is quilted with bubbles instead of scales (Fish Tales 6).

If you look at the bottom of the quilt, you will find Bubblejoy's grandma (Fish Tales 7) quilted in bubbles also. What she lacks in gradation she makes up for with her beautiful matte bubbles.

2 There are some wispy plants quilted on the bottom of the quilt. They reach for the sun in various places. Other areas are air bubbles floating to the surface.

3 The quilting is overall very subtle. If you want it splashier, use a contrasting or metallic thread. The quilting will be more visible and become a stronger character in the story.

Fish Tales 5

Heather's Halos

This quilt has been a very long time in the making. Many years ago, my family suffered an incredible loss. My cousin Heather was in an automobile accident that claimed her life. She was too young and we loved her far too much for this to happen.

Since that time, our family has experienced more loss and sorrow. Heather has been with us through those times—I have felt her. I longed to create a tribute to her and designed this angel. But I never was able to put it in a complete quilt. The design wasn't right or the fabrics weren't right. The angel block got put in a stack of quilt ideas and waited for me to be ready.

Now, the block has resurfaced and demands to be utilized. The image of Heather all around our family, holding and supporting us, is finally taking shape. I miss my cousin desperately, but can now remember her with beauty and charm instead of focusing on the prospect of our lives continuing without her. Her life was a gift to our family, and it is time to share her with you.

Heather's Halos

Finished Quilt: 36½" × 48"
Pieced and quilted by the author
Black-and-white prints courtesy of Marcus Brothers Textiles.
Batiks courtesy of Bali Fabrics.

materials

Background Fabric: 2 ¾ yards light, tone-on-tone white

Light purple patterned batik: ¼ yard

Medium purple batik: ⅛ yard

Dark purple batik silk: ¾ yard

Rusty orange silk: ⅛ yard

Light peach batik fabric: ⅛ yard

Dark black with white print: ½ yard

Medium dark black with white print: ½ yard

Medium black with white print: ½ yard

Medium light black with white print: ½ yard

Binding Fabric: ⅔ yard dark black with silver

Backing: 1½ yards

Batting: 44 ½" × 56"

Foundation Fabric: 11 yards of 12" wide foundation

Sulky Iron-On Transfer Pen

Several sheet white paper 8½" × 11"

Fabric Suggestions

Choose a pure simple white-on-white fabric for the background. You could use a solid white if it is a brilliant white. This background needs to glow and not lay flat.

Batiks work beautifully for wings because of their lovely patterns. Choose slightly different values to differentiate the foreground wings from the background wings.

Have fun choosing a beautiful silk for Heather's dress. Let it shine!

Play with different scales and print types for the wing border. Let the wings climb upward with changing value.

cutting list

Strips are cut across the width of the fabric unless otherwise stated.

From Background Fabric:
    Cut 1 strip 6½", then from this strip, cut the following:
        2 strips 6½" × 10"
        4 strips 6½" × 5¼"
    Cut 2 strips 5"
    Cut 2 strips 4"
    Cut 2 strip 3½"
    Cut 6 strips 3"
    Cut 9 strips 2½"
    Cut 3 strips 2"
    Cut 3 strips 1½"

From Light Purple Patterned Batik:
    Cut 1 strip 4"

From Medium Purple Batik:
    Cut 2 strips 1½"

From Dark Purple Batik Silk:
    Cut 2 strips 3¾"
    Cut 9 strips 1¾"

From Rusty Orange Silk:
    Cut 1 strip 1"

From Light Peach Batik Fabric:
    Cut 1 strip 1¼", then from this strip, cut the following:
        9 squares 1¼" × 1¼"

From Dark Black With White Print:
    Cut 3 strips 5"

From Medium Dark Black With White Print:
    Cut 3 strips 4½"

From Medium Black With White Print:
    Cut 3 strips 4½"

From Medium Light Black With White Print:
    Cut 3 strips 4"

From Binding Fabric:
    Cut 1 square 21" × 21" to make 2¼" continuous bias binding

From Foundation Fabric:
    Cut 9 rectangles 8" x 12" for angels

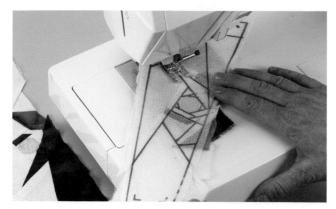

Heather's Halos 1

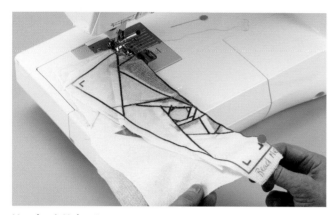

Heather's Halos 2

Heather's Halos 3

Heather's Halos 4

Preparation

1 With the iron-on transfer pen, trace the 2 sections of Heather onto a sheet of white 8½" × 11" paper. Put dots in the corners of the seams that will be joined; this will aid in piecing later on. Heat-transfer 9 copies of each half onto foundation fabric.

2 With the iron-on transfer pen, trace the 4 sections of border wings onto sheets of paper. Mark the corners of the seams with dots to aid with perpendicular pinning. Heat-transfer 17 copies of each section onto foundation fabric.

3 Heat transfer the wing sections onto the long foundation strip, leaving just a little space between each. (Cutting rectangles before you transfer the pattern would just waste foundation.) After tracing all 17 copies of each section, cut each section apart just outside the transferred line.

Piecing the Blocks

1 Foundation piece the Heather halves according to the fabric and number key on the foundation patterns. Start with the peach square and piece that half first (Heather's Halos 1). You will be glad to have that half done!

2 After you have pieced all of the halo halves, tackle the wings. They will come together quickly and easily. Press each half block.

3 Trim on the cutting line of all of the blocks and layer the half blocks right sides together to make a complete angel block.

4 Perpendicularly pin through the corresponding dots in the upper and lower corners of the sections, then sew the seam (Heather's Halos 2). Press the seam open. Repeat to make a total of 9 angels blocks. Square each block to 6½" x 10".

5 Foundation piece the 4 sections of the wings. Experiment with chain piecing the same section of each block. Go right down the strip of black print fabric with the foundation pattern on top. Keep sewing and cut the strip apart later (Heather's Halos 3).

6 If you chain pieced some sections, take the strip to the ironing board and set the seam and press the fabrics open before cutting the sections apart. After pressing, scissor cut roughly outside the transferred line (Heather's Halos 4), and get ready to add the next piece!

7 Continue to piece all the sections of the wings. Press all the sections and cut accurately on the cutting lines to be joined.

8 Perpendicularly pin and start joining the darkest wing section to the next section. Keep the rhythm by adding the sections in order and in a chain. The piecing will go more quickly, and we love to see progress!

9 Press the seams. After all 4 sections are joined in all 17 wing blocks, give them a final press. Square each block to 6½" × 10".

Assembling the Quilt Center

1 Sew 2 Angel blocks together to make a vertical unit. Repeat to make a total of 3 vertical units.

2 Sew a 6½" × 10" background rectangle to the top of 1 vertical unit from step 1. Press all the seams one way. This is vertical Row 4.

3 Sew a 6½" × 10" background rectangle in between 2 individual angel blocks, vertically, and press all the seams one way. This is vertical Row 2.

4 To make vertical Row 1, add a 6½" × 5¼" background rectangle to the top and one to the bottom of a 2 vertical unit from step 1. Press all the seams one way. Repeat to make vertical Row 3.

5 Stitch Row 1 to Row 2 side by side. Stitch Row 3 to Row 4 side by side. Stitch Row 2 to Row 3. Press all the seams to one side.

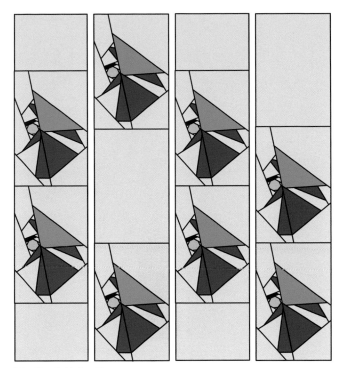

Heather's Halos 5

Heather's Halos 6

Heather's Halos 7

Creating the Borders

1 Sew 2 wing blocks together with the darkest wing in the upper position. Repeat to make a total of 4 pairs of wing blocks.

2 Join 1 pair from step 1 to another pair from step 1, maintaining the upper position of the darkest section (Heather's Halos 6). Repeat to make a second strip of 4 wing blocks. Press all the seams to one side.

3 Sew 1 wing block unit with the darkest wing at the bottom left next to 1 wing block with the darkest wing still at the top right (Heather's Halos 7).

4 Sew this new unit to the far right end of the 4-block unit from step 2 that has been flipped to have the darkest wing on the bottom. This is the bottom border (Heather's Halos 8). Press all the seams in one direction.

5 Sew 1 angel block to the right-hand side of a wing block with the darkest wing at the bottom left (Heather's Halos 9).

6 Sew 1 unit from step 2, with the darkest wings at the top right, to the right-hand side of the angel in the pair you made in step 5. This is the top border (Heather's Halos 10). Press all the seams to one side.

7 With the 6 remaining wing blocks, make 2 vertical rows of 3 blocks each. Maintain the darkest wing in the same upper position in all 3 blocks of each row. These are the side borders (Heather's Halos 11). Press all the seams one way.

Heather's Halos 8

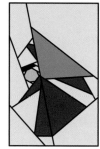

Heather's Halos 9

Heather's Halos 10

Heather's Halos 11

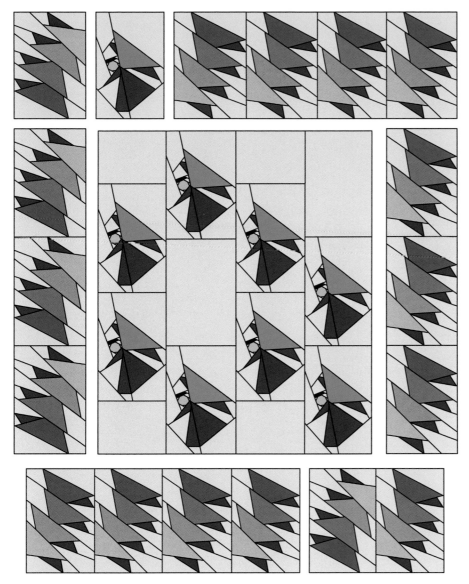

Heather's Halos 12

Adding the Borders

1 Sew 1 side border to the right-hand side of the quilt center, with the darkest wings at the top of each block.

2 Sew the remaining side border to the left side of the quilt center, with the darkest wings at the bottom of each block. Press seams out.

3 Sew the bottom border onto the bottom of the quilt center with the flipped block on the far right. Press the seams out.

4 Sew the top border onto the top of the quilt center, with the angel flying right side up. Press the seams out.

You can't say that this was hard. It might have been time-consuming, but it certainly wasn't hard. All good things take time. You made it, and look what you have to show for your efforts! Way to go!

Layering, Quilting, and Binding

1 Get ready to send Heather flying on some wispy quilted air currents. Maybe you will quilt "unseen" angels in the negative spaces in the quilt. Whatever you choose, enjoy the process and take time to breathe.

Thank you for taking this personal journey with me. Creating, quilting and healing are one in the same.

Beauty is subjective. Not everyone admires the oddly shaped tree or the slightly wilted blossom. Hair askance can mar the perfect portrait for some, but for others it evokes the beauty of being human. Nature is full of opportunities to notice, appreciate and celebrate.

Much of my fascination with trees, and evergreens in particular, is their complete unpredictability and nonconformity. Each specimen is what it is—no more and no less. How we perceive it is the challenge and the adventure. Nurturing unique and struggling trees brings me so much satisfaction. I relish their perseverance and courage in spite of being misunderstood and shunned. I celebrate their daily growth and encourage their "wild arms" as signs of independence and strength. Nature is natural and *Bleautry* honors all trees that stand maligned yet proud in spite of their perceived limitations. Straight and tall or twisted and small, *Bleautry* salutes them all.

Bleautry
Finished Quilt: 43" × 43
Pieced and quilted by the author

materials

Background Fabric: 1 yard light color

Outer Border and Tree Fabric: 1½ yards textured black-on-black stripe

Binding, Inner Border, and Tree Fabric: ⅞ yard small-scale black-on-black

Textured Black Fabrics: ⅛ yard of each of 6 fabrics, such as velvet, corduroy, silk, cotton, brocade, textured cotton

Zinger Fabric: ¼ yard clear blue

Backing: 1½ yards

Batting: 51" × 51"

Foundation Fabric: 1 yard of 20" wide foundation

Fabric Suggestions

Pull out those garment fabric scraps to get a vast array of black textures. (The photo here is overexposed to show texture.)

Use a clear, distinct blue to set off this quilt, and choose a background with a lot of interest—we see a big hunk of it!

cutting list

Strips are cut across the width of the fabric unless otherwise stated.

From Background Fabric:
  Cut 1 strip 17½", then from this strip, cut the following:
    2 squares 17½" × 17½", then cut each in half once, corner to corner to make a total of 4 triangles
  Cut 1 strip 8"
  Cut 2 strips 3½"

From Outer Border and Tree Fabric:
  Cut 2 strips 25", then from these strips, cut the following:
    2 squares 25" × 25", then cut each in half once, corner to corner to make a total of 4 triangles

From Binding, Inner Border and Tree Fabric:
  Cut 1 square 22" × 22" for continuous 2¼" bias binding
  Cut 4 strips 1½", then from these strips, cut the following:
    2 strips 1½" × 24½"
    2 strips 1½" × 27½"

From Zinger Fabric:
  Cut 4 strips 1¼", then from these strips, cut the following:
    4 strips 1¼" × 27½"

From Foundation Fabric:
  Cut 1 rectangle 14" x 28"

Bleautry 1

Bleautry 2

Bleautry 3

Preparation

1 Line up the stately pine pattern into one long "bleautiful" tree, and tape it together for stability.

2 Trace the pine pattern, in its entirety, onto 14" x 28" foundation rectangle for foundation piecing. Do not put the numbers in the background sections, as they may show through the finished quilt. Also, trace each section of the tree individually, leaving approximately ½" around each section.

3 Cut out each section ½" outside the traced line. These individual foundations will be used to "pre-piece" the tree sections for a crazy patch look.

4 Prepare 2¼" continuous bias binding with the 22" × 22" square of binding, and set it aside.

Piecing Individual Sections of Pine

1 Layer the foundation (with the traced line down) with 1 fabric strip right side up.

2 Fold back an approximately ½" lengthwise seam allowance on another strip, and place it on top of the first strip, right side up (Bleautry 2).

3 Using a fun thread and a decorative stitch, topstitch the second strip in place to secure both strips (Bleautry 3). Continue adding strips until the foundation section is covered.

4 Trim the sections to the foundation edge (not to the traced line) after all the strips are added.

5 Add interest by varying strip widths and placement angles as well as using different decorative stitches (Bleautry 3).

Completing the Pine

1 Using the pre-pieced foundation section for the tree fabric and the pre-cut background strips, foundation piece the entire pine according to the number sequence on the foundation pattern. Press the completed pine.

2 Trim the pine block to 12½" × 26½".

3 Using a square ruler, trim the corners from the top of the block to create a 90-degree point (Bleautry 4).

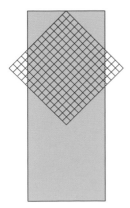

Bleautry 4

4 Retrieve 3 triangles cut from the 17½" background squares. (You will have 1 extra.) Add a triangle to each side of the pine block. Press the seam allowances out.

5 Add the remaining triangle to the bottom of the block and press the seam down. Square the block to 24½" × 24½".

Adding the Inner Border

1 Sew a 2" × 24½" inner border strip to opposite sides of the square pine block, and press the seam allowances out.

2 Sew a 2" × 27½" inner border strip to each remaining side of the pine block. Press the seams out.

Adding the Zinger Border

1 Fold each 1¼" x 27½" zinger strip in half lengthwise (wrong sides together) and press.

2 Matching raw edges, sew a zinger strip to opposite sides of the block with a 1/8" seam allowance. Do not press.

3 Sew a strip to each remaining side of the block. Be careful to keep the zinger strips flat underneath the strip you are adding. Do not press.

Adding the Outer Border

1 Retrieve the 4 triangles cut from the 25" outer border squares and sew a triangle to opposite sides of the pine block. Press the seams out. Be careful to keep the zinger border flat toward the middle.

2 Sew a triangle to each of the remaining sides, and press the seam allowances out. Be careful to keep the zinger border flat toward the middle. Square the entire quilt top to 43" × 43".

Layering, Quilting and Binding

1 Remember, after you quilt your fabulous *Bleautry*, the binding is all ready to put on. What a treat that is!

2 Use metallic thread to dress up the quilting in the large dark outer border. The simple grid design adds sparkle without taking focus from the spectacular pine.

3 Hope you enjoyed this adventure! Keep planting those pines— *Bleautry* can help you go "green!"

Bleautry 5

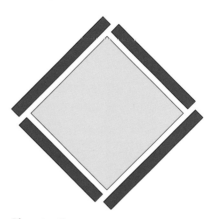

Bleautry 6

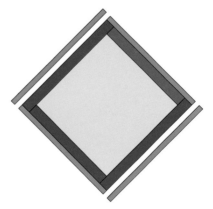

Bleautry 7

Sweet Liberty, Too

S*weet Liberty, Too* was a challenging quilt to make. While it's not technically difficult, the subject matter made it a quilt that would be made in its own time. I started it and put it down several times before it was clear to me what the end result would be.

My husband has been in the Army Reserves for as long as I have known him. The threat of a deployment was always a possibility, but not one we dwelled on. Unfortunately, the threat became a reality in 2004. He had to leave his wife and four children in a new home—which he had lived in for only two weeks—for a year-long "sand vacation" in Iraq.

Sweet Liberty, Too is my tribute to our year of separation. My husband, the soldier, is at the very center of the quilt. Though he is separated from us by distance and duty, his children encompass him with their sunshine and love. I found the most incredible vintage fabric that embodied that joy; it's the border supporting our soldier. There is necessary space between the children's borders and the stars and stripes of the "Momma" border. My job was to see that my children flourished, despite the sadness and uncertainty. And if this sounds like I was the one holding it all together, look again—the sunshine of the children are the ultimate framework of the entire quilt.

The children are truly my heroes. They brought joy and immense love to our lives throughout that year. *Sweet Liberty, Too* celebrates their victory. They have persevered.

Sweet Liberty, Too
Finished Quilt: 69" × 84"
Pieced and quilted by the author

materials

Frame and Outer Border Fabric: 2 ⅓ yards medium-value large-scale black, white and yellow print

First Separation Border Fabric: ⅞ yard light, white-on-white print

Second Separation Border Fabric: 1¾ yards a different light white-on-white print

Background Piecing Fabric: ⅝ yard light, white-on-white print

Soldier Star Fabric: ⅓ yard dark black solid (the darkest value in the quilt)

Momma Stars and Stripes Fabric: 2 yards very light, white-on-white print and 12 fat quarters dark to medium-dark black with white prints in varying scales

Binding Fabric: ⅞ yard small-scale medium black and white ging-ham check

Backing: 5 yards light, white-on-white print

Sulky Iron-On Transfer Pen

Foundation Fabric: 3½ yards of 20" wide foundation

2 pieces of white paper 8½" × 11"

Pencil

Fabric Suggestions

Choose fabrics that are similar in value, but have scale varia-tions for the dark Momma Stars & Stripes. Keep the values close; too much fluctuation in the "support system" fabrics would detract from the strength of the design.

The three background fabrics should have the same value but can differ in scale. You could even use the same fabric for all three sections. Using the same value for all three helps the Soldier Star float in the center and yet remain connected to the rest of the quilt. The Soldier Star fabric should be the darkest and most intense. A solid or tone-on-tone fabric would be great. For the Outer Border, use a strong and graphic print with just enough color to make the quilt sing.

cutting list

Strips are cut across the width of the fabric unless otherwise stated.

From the Frame and Outer Border Fabric:
    Cut 2 *lengthwise* strips 8½" × 68"
    Cut 2 *lengthwise* strips 8½" × 69"
    Cut 2 strips 2" × 14¼"
    Cut 2 strips 2" × 22" strips

From the First Separation Border Fabric:
    Cut 3 strips 5", then from these strips, cut the following:
        Cut 2 strips 5" × 25"
        Cut 1 strip 5" × 23"
    Cut 1 strip 9", then from this strip, cut the following:
        Cut 1 strip 9" × 23"

From the Second Separation Border Fabric:
    Cut 4 *lengthwise* strips 8" × 53"

From the Background Piecing Fabric:
    Cut 1 strip 10"
    Cut 1 strip 7"

From the Soldier Star Fabric:
    Cut 1 strip 8"

From the Dark Momma Stars & Stripes Fabrics:
    Cut 1 strip 5"
    Cut 3 strips 1¾"

From the Light Momma Stars & Stripes Fabric:
    Cut 7 strips 4"
    Cut 15 strips 1¾"

From the Binding Fabric:
    Cut 1 square 28" × 28" to make 2¼" continuous bias binding

From the Foundation Fabric:
    Cut 1 rectangle 20" × 24"
    Cut 20 squares 9" × 9"

Sweet Liberty, Too 1

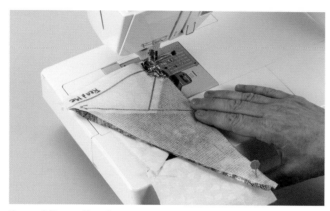

Sweet Liberty, Too 2

Sweet Liberty, Too 3

Sweet Liberty, Too 4

Preparation

1 Using an iron-on transfer pen, trace 1 copy of the Momma Star sections and Momma Stripes foundation patterns onto a piece of white paper.

2 Heat-transfer the patterns onto the 9" foundation squares. Repeat until you have 10 of each foundation pattern. If the transferred ink becomes too faint to see easily, retrace the existing lines with the iron-on transfer pen and start ironing again.

3 Enlarge the Soldier Star Foundation Pattern by 225 percent to make it measure 11" × 22". I added fudge room around the Soldier Star to trim off later when we square up the block.

4 Using a pencil, trace 1 copy of each of the Soldier Star units directly onto the rectangle of foundation fabric.

Piecing the Stars and Stripes

1 Foundation piece the 3 Soldier Star sections. Refer to the numbers and fabric guide on the foundation pattern for fabric placement and piecing order (Sweet Liberty, Too 1).

2 Press the sections, and cut neatly on the cutting lines where the sections will be joined.

3 Using perpendicular pinning, sew Section A to Section B; this is Section AB (Sweet Liberty Too 2). Press the seam allowance toward Section B.

4 Join Section C to Section AB (from step 3). Press the seam toward Section C. Press well, and trim to 11" × 22". Set the Soldier Star aside.

5 Foundation piece the Momma Star sections to make 10 of each Momma Star section. Use 1 fabric for all 3 sections of each star. Press, trim, and join the 3 sections of each Momma Star . Make a total of 10 Momma Star blocks.

6 Foundation piece the Momma Stripes blocks, making a total of 10 blocks (Sweet Liberty, Too 3). Use an assortment of the fabrics for the stripes. Don't be afraid to mix it up!

7 Press the Momma Star and Momma Stripe blocks, and square each to 8" × 8". I just love not having to remove foundations after I'm done stitching!

Assembling the Rows

1 Using 3 Momma Stars and 2 Momma Stripes Blocks for each row, make 2 horizontal rows (Sweet Liberty, Too 4). Sew the blocks together, alternating stars and stripes. Press the seam allowances to one side.

2 Using 3 Momma Stripes and 2 Momma Stars blocks for each row, make 2 vertical rows. Sew the blocks together, alternating the stripes and stars. Press the seams to one side.

Assembling the Top

1 Sew the a 2" × 22" frame strip to each 22" side of the Soldier Star. Press the seam allowances out.

2 Sew a 2" × 14¼" frame strip to the top and another to the bottom of the Soldier Star. Press the seam allowances out.

3 Sew a 5" x 25" separation strip to each side of the quilt center. Press the seams out toward the separation strips.

4 Sew the 5" × 23" separation strip to the top of the quilt center. Press the seams out.

5 Sew the 9" × 23" separation strip to the bottom of the quilt center.

6 Sew the vertical Momma Stars & Stripes row to each side of the quilt center. Press the seams toward the separation strips.

7 Sew a Momma Stars & Stripes horizontal rows to the top and to the bottom of the quilt center. Press the seams toward the separation strips.

8 Sew an 8" × 53" second separation strip to each side of the quilt center. Press the seams toward the separations strips.

9 Sew the 8" × 53" second separation strips to the top and to the bottom of the quilt center. Press the seams out toward the strip.

10 Add an 8½" × 68" outer border strips to each side of the quilt center. Press the seams out.

11 Add the 8½" × 69" border strips to the top and to the bottom of the quilt center. Press the seams out.

Layering, Quilting and Binding

1 This quilt is a good candidate for long-arm quilting. It is large enough to be unwieldy and unhandy on your home sewing machine, unless you are a whiz at manipulating bulky quilts.

2 I chose to quilt the words of Abraham Lincoln. I selected 3 quotes that were especially fitting for Gary and his separation from us.

3 I included stars and sections of strong straight lines. The Soldier Star in the center is quilted in bubbles, signifying the kids' love keeping Gary afloat.

4 If you prefer hand quilting, a simple crosshatch in the separation strips and some stitch in the ditch in the Momma Stars & Stripes would be beautiful.

5 Remember to end with snazzy binding and to label or sign your quilt.

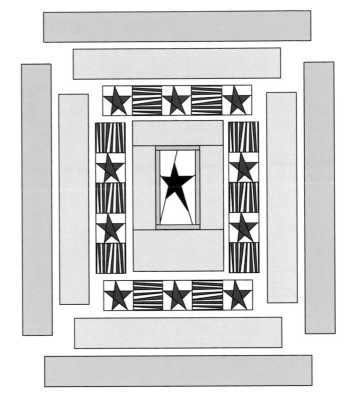

Sweet Liberty, Too 5

Joy is simple. Joy is elemental. It can't be taught, and it can't be imitated. The real thing is bliss beyond compare. I see it in my children's eyes. I feel it in their touch and hear it in their laughter. Joy sings and dances and celebrates. This quilt marks that feeling and provides a creative outlet to join in the party. Make merry while piecing a tribute to joy in all of our lives.

Joy!

Finished Quilt: 17" × 17"
Pieced and quilted by the author
Black-and-white fabric courtesy of Avlyn, Inc.
Yellow batik fabric courtesy of Robert Kaufman Fabrics

materials

Background Fabric: ⅓ yard light white textured solid fabric

Lettering Fabric: ⅛ yard white-on-black polka dot

Piecing and Inner Border Fabric: ¼ yard dark, white-on-black, small-scale print

Piecing Fabric: ¼ yard light, black-on-white, large-scale print

Border Fabric: ⅛ yard dark, white-on-black, large-scale print

Cornerstone Fabric: ⅛ yard vibrant yellow

Binding Fabric: ½ yard dark, white-on-black print

Foundation Fabric: ½ yard of 12" wide foundation

Backing: ⅔ yard light, white-on-white fabric

Batting: 21" × 21"

Fabric Suggestions

I used a small-scale, white-on-white polka-dot for the background. Nothing says "fun" like polka-dots! The lettering is done with an even smaller scale white-on-black polka-dot. The piecing uses a larger dragonfly print and sparkly star print to step out to the larger-scale and irregular white-on-black polka-dot border. The intense yellow zinger fabric frames and sparks the simple design to life. The snazzy binding is done with a white-on-black plaid on the bias.

cutting list

Strips are cut across the width of the fabric unless otherwise stated.

From Background Fabric:
    Cut 1 strip 3½"
    Cut 1 strip 2½"
    Cut 1 strip 2", then from this strip cut the following:
        1 strip 2" × 9½"
    Cut 1 strip 1½", then from this strip cut the following:
        1 strip 1½" × 7½"
        1 square 1½" × 1½"

From Lettering Fabric:
    Cut 2 strips 2"

From Dark Piecing and Inner Border Fabric:
    Cut 4 strips 1½", then from these strips cut the following:
        2 strips 1½" × 12½"
        2 strips 1½" × 14½"
        2 squares 1½" × 1½"

From Light Piecing Fabric:
    Cut 3 strips 1½", then from these strips cut the following:
        1 strip 1½" × 6½"
        1 strip 1½" × 3½"
        1 strip 1½" × 2½"

From Border Fabric:
    Cut 1 strip 3", then from this strip cut the following:
        1 strip 3" × 14¼"
        1 strip 2½" × 17"

From Cornerstone Fabric:
    Cut 2 strips 1¼", then from these strips cut the following:
        4 strips 1¼" × 14½"

From Binding Fabric:
    Cut 1 square 14" × 14" for 2¼" continuous bias binding

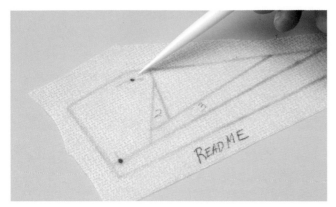

Joy! 1

Preparation

1 Using a pencil, trace 1 copy of each Joy foundation section directly onto the foundation fabric. Leave a little space between the sections when tracing.

2 Mark the numbers in the *j, o* and *y* to aid in piecing. Since the foundation can stay in the quilt and the background is lighter fabric, don't mark the numbers on the background sections. I don't want to risk having the numbers show through the background.

3 Mark the corners with a dot to help when you join the sections later (Joy! 1). Cut just outside of the traced lines to separate the sections.

Piecing the Joy

1 Foundation piece each of the 5 sections, one by one. Press all of the sections, and carefully trim on the cutting line.

2 Layer Section 1 and Section 2 right sides together.

3 Put a pin through the center of the dot marking the top corner of Section 2 and the matching corner of Section 1. Keep it perpendicular to the fabric to inhibit shifting (Joy! 2).

4 Perpendicularly pin the other facing corners of Section 1 and Section 2. Stitch the sections together and press the seam open.

5 Join Section 3 to the unit from step 4, making sure to perpendicularly pin the corners to reduce shifting. Press the seam open.

6 Continue adding sections and pressing until all are joined and all seams are pressed open (Joy! 3).

7 Square the Joy block to 6" × 9½" (Joy 4).

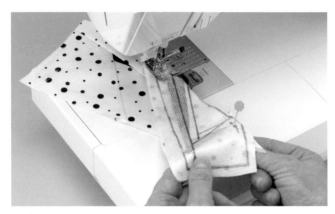

Joy! 2

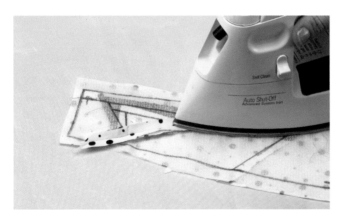

Joy! 3

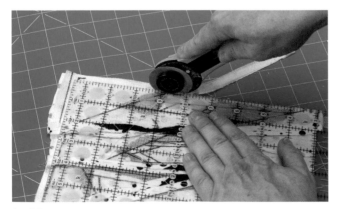

Joy! 4

Creating the 9-Patches

1 You will piece 9-patch blocks for the checkerboard piecing. Cut 2 light 1½" piecing strips in half, yielding 4 strips about 1½" × 21". Repeat with 2 dark 1½" piecing strips.

2 Sew a dark strip from step 1 and a light strip from step 1 together lengthwise. Repeat once for a total of 2 sets. Press the seams toward the dark strip.

3 Join a dark strip from step 1 to the light strip from a set from step 2. Press the seam toward the dark strip (Joy! 5).

4 Join a light strip from step 1 to the dark strip of the other set from step 2. Press the seam toward the dark strip.

5 Layer the strip sets from step 3 and 4 right sides together, and nestle the seam allowances. Press the layered strip sets (Joy! 6).

6 Transfer the strip sets from step 5 to the cutting table, and cut 10 segments, each 1½" wide (Joy! 7).

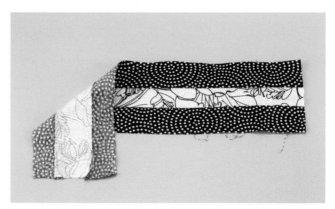

Joy! 5

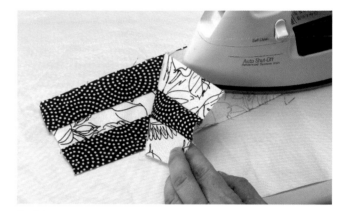

Joy! 6

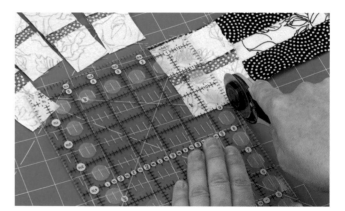

Joy! 7

Joy! 8

7 Do not separate the segment pairs. Transfer them to the left of the sewing machine. Stitch 1 segment pair together side by side (not end to end). Repeat for each of 5 more segment pairs. Press the seams toward the strip with the most dark squares. Separate the other 4 segment pairs.

8 Stack 3 stitched units from step 7 with a light square in the upper-left position. Stitch separated pair strip with 2 light squares to the right-hand side of each unit to complete the 9-patch (Joy! 9). Press the seam allowances in toward the center strip.

9 Stack 3 stitched units from step 7 with a dark square in the upper left position. Stitch a separated pair strip with 2 dark squares to the right-hand side of each units to complete the 9-patch (Joy! 10). Press the seam allowances out toward the darker strips.

10 Sort the 9-patches from steps 8 and 9 into 2 piles of like blocks. Stitch a dark-cornered 9-patch to the right-hand side of a light-cornered 9-patch (Joy! 11). Repeat to make a total of 3 block sets. Press the seam allowances toward the darker strips.

11 Join 2 block sets to make a row of 4 blocks and press (Joy! 12). Set aside.

Joy! 9

Joy! 10

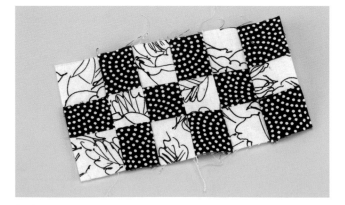

Joy! 11

Assembling the Top

1 To assemble the top, you will add spacer strips and the 9-patches around the Joy block. Begin by stitching the 2" × 9½" background strip to the right-hand side of the Joy block. Press the seam allowances toward the strip.

2 Stitch the 1½" × 1½" background square to a dark 1½" × 1½" piecing square. Press the seam toward the black square.

3 Onto the other side of the black square from step 2, add the 1½" × 7½" background strip. Press the seams toward the black square.

4 With the squares at the top, join the strip from step 3 vertically to the left side of the Joy block (Joy! 13). Press the seam out toward the strip.

5 Stitch the remaining 1½"-wide separated segment pair (with 2 dark) squares (from step 7 under Creating the 9-Patches) to the 1½" × 6½" light piecing strip. Press the seam toward the black square. With the squares on top and matching the seams, join the strip vertically to the left side of the Joy block (Joy! 14). Press the seam out toward the strip.

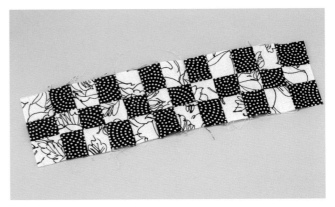

Joy! 12

Joy! 13

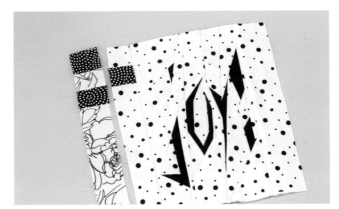

Joy! 14

Joy! 15

Joy! 16

Joy! 17

6 Join the other dark 1½" × 1½" piecing square to the end of the 1½" × 2½" light piecing strip. Press the seam toward the black square. With the square on the bottom, join this strip to the remaining 1½"-wide separated pair segment with 2 light squares. Press the seam allowance toward the strip. Add the light 1½" × 3½" piecing strip to the right-hand side of the strip, making a faux 9-patch. Press the seam toward the strip.

7 Rights sides together, nestle the seams of the faux 9-patch strip to the end of the remaining 2-block unit (from step 10 under Creating the 9-Patches) to continue the alternating pattern. Press the seam, and stitch this unit to the bottom of the Joy block, with the faux block on the right. Press the seam up toward the block.

8 Retrieve the 4-block 9-patch strip (from step 11 under Creating the 9-Patches). With right sides together, match the seams and join the 9-patch strip to the left side of the quilt center. A dark square will be in the lower-left corner. Press the seam out toward the 9-patches.

Adding the Borders

1 You will be adding the inner border, a cornerstone border, and an asymmetrical border to the quilt center. Begin by sewing a 1½" × 12½" dark inner border strip to the top and bottom of the quilt center and one to the bottom. Press the seams out.

2 Sew a 1½" × 14½" inner border strip to each side of the quilt center (Joy! 18). Press the seams out.

3 Press the 1¼" × 14½" cornerstone border strips in half lengthwise, wrong sides together. Lining up all raw edges, stitch a strip to the top and one to the bottom of the quilt center with a ⅛" seam allowance. Do not press this cornerstone border out! Keeping the border flat and in toward the center, add a remaining cornerstone strip to each side of the quilt center (Joy! 19). Do not press out.

4 Stitch the 3" × 14½" border strip to the bottom of the quilt center. Sandwich the cornerstone border in between the inner border and the outer border with all edges matching. Press the outer border out without pressing the cornerstone border out.

5 Stitch the 2½" × 17" border strip to the left of the quilt center. Sandwich the cornerstone border in between the inner border and the outer border with all edges matching. Press the outer border out without pressing the cornerstone border out.

6 Your quilt top is finished! Feel the joy!

Finishing the Quilt

1 Layer and quilt this beauty however you desire. I used a tight, random grid in the text block to add dimension and shading to the simple white background. This dense quilting pops *Joy!* right off the quilt.

2 A wavy diagonal grid lends a contrasting old-fashioned element to the contemporary quilting in the text block, and a licorice whip quilted in the inner border helps the cornerstone border fly freely between the borders. Simple grids on the outer border complete the mixed bag of motifs on this small but mighty quilt.

Joy! 18

Joy! 19

Joy! 20

How Do I Deal With "Opportunities"?

In spite of our best intentions and preplanning, some surprises do crop up as we foundation piece. Even though we start with strips and check the perimeter and do all of those other helpful things, occasionally we wind up with an "oops." Please notice that I did not say "mistake." *Mistake* is not a word in the vocabulary of a stress-free foundation piecer. What we have is a series of opportunities that provide a wealth of creative choices. Let's look at some of those "opportunities" in detail.

Strip Too Narrow

The pattern called for a certain size strip to cover the section. Oops! It doesn't seem to cover the whole section. This provides a few choices and opportunities for you.

Opportunity Number 1

To create a wider strip, you could lift up the strip and join another strip to it (right sides together) while it is flapping free. Press the seam allowance to one side, and you are ready to keep piecing! If your project is scrappy and you are really adventurous, you could add a different fabric strip to cover the section.

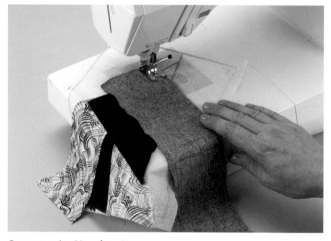

Opportunity Number 2

Another option is to add a strip and stitch through all three layers as you would for normal foundation piecing. This method keeps you in the rhythm of not stitching unless there are three layers.

To make this creative choice, you will need to stitch on the fabric side of the piece instead of the foundation side. Keeping the foundation up would make it very difficult to see what you are doing and could create yet another "opportunity"!

Once again, the creative choice is yours as to whether you add the same fabric or a different one to completely cover the section.

Opportunity Number 3

Perhaps this opportunity happened because you felt the designer of the pattern didn't truly understand the section you were adding. According to your artistic sensibilities, the designer put the line in the wrong place. The bottom of the tree wants to be a little narrower or shorter or whatever your creative muse says.

I have found that my students are very considerate and caring when they feel I've designed something with a line in the wrong place for their version. Instead of just telling me my design is wrong, they often use this opportunity to move the line without offending me. This method lets you redraw the stitching line to suit your sensibilities and eliminate the need to choose between Opportunities 1 and 2. My patterns are just starting points, so by all means, listen to your muse!

Opportunity Number 4

This opportunity opens the door to texture, as well. Seams add texture and change how light plays on the surface of the quilt. How very clever of you to make a textural statement by adding another seam line to the design.

Foundation Peeking Through

Y ou have finished a block, and now you see that on one of the first sections a corner of foundation is peeking through where you would have expected it to be covered with the strip. This provides many artistic choices.

Opportunity Number 1
Depending on the design, you could simply add a button or embellishment over the naked corner. Every tree needs a bird, right?

Opportunity Number 2
Since you have been foundation piecing, you have neglected your appliqué skills. In order to hone those skills, appliqué a bit of fabric over the empty spot. It could be the same fabric, or you could use a different one if the block is scrappy.

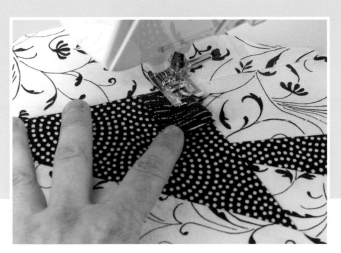

Opportunity Number 3

Another skill we have been neglecting is topstitching. You could topstitch over the naked corner a piece of fabric, with its edges turned under ⅛" to ¼". This is great practice, and you could even use a decorative stitch with this method.

Opportunity Number 4

We haven't practiced coloring in awhile, have we? You know those Pigma pens you bought and haven't used yet? Now is the time! Dig them out, and color in that little naked spot. This is one of the things they make Pigma pens for—isn't it on the packaging? We are so creative, aren't we?!

Opportunity Number 5

If you notice the bare spot right away as it happens, you can just stitch a deeper seam to cover the nakedness.

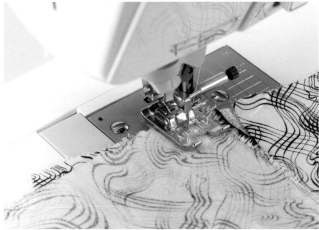

Opportunity Number 6

If a bare spot occurs and your strip isn't wide enough to reseam, just add another strip on a new line that encompasses the bare spot. No broken threads needed here! Leave the bottom strip in for a bit of texture. You could also trim a bit of it away if you aren't comfortable with leaving the extra layer intact.

Added Texture

W e have touched on the importance of texture in our work. Sometimes my designs won't add enough for your tastes. When that happens, you might see a tuck in a seam. This creative choice opens many doors for experimenting and growing.

Opportunity Number 1

If the tuck is in a tree branch, perhaps a bird—or a nest—or an owl—needs to sit in there!

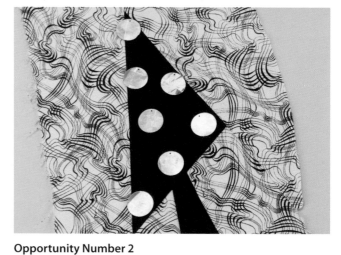

Opportunity Number 2

You intended to embellish your project all along, this lovely flap gives you the perfect spot to gather it up with beads or sequins.

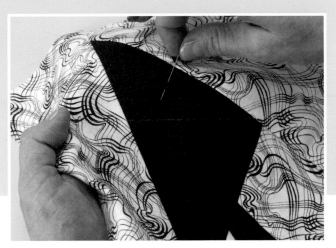

Opportunity Number 3

If you are my 92-year-old grandma, you will reach for a needle and thread and finely tack the tuck down with beautifully hidden stitches. You go, girl!

Opportunity Number 4

You could do more practice with your topstitching skills and topstitch the little flap down.

Opportunity Number 5

If you are really daring, you will let the tuck flap in the wind, and watch it play as you quilt it. You could also let your machine quilter decorate it when it is quilted!

Opportunity Number 6

If you are looking for even more texture, simply add another section on top of the tuck. Leave all of the layers there, and watch the light play on the surface. Whatever creative avenue you choose, you certainly do not need to remove any stitches! Leave those precious little things alone!

Wrong Side of the Fabric

We have seen the price of fabric rise throughout the years. How clever of you to get more bang for your buck by using both sides of the fabric! Two for the price of one!

However, if this creative leap makes you nervous or uncomfortable, I have some wonderful ideas for you that don't involve a seam ripper!

Opportunity Number 1

If the flipped fabric is very close in value on both sides (perhaps a white-on-white fabric) I encourage you to do nothing at all! Take the creative leap to let your quilt happen as it happens.

Opportunity Number 2

If the quilt is scrappy and the flipped patch is close in value to the other pieces, I challenge you to leave it be!

Opportunity Number 3

If the patch is not quite close enough in value or needs more design, pull out the Pigma pens and practice drawing! (Permanent markers work, too, but they soak through more.)

Opportunity Number 4

You could add another fabric on top of the flipped piece if you aren't comfortable leaving it alone. Don't take the time to unsew it; just slap another piece over it and use topstitching or whatever you choose to secure the patch.

Blocks Smaller Than the Pattern

here is a very good reason why I wait to square my blocks up until all of them are pieced. I want to get the most bang for my buck!

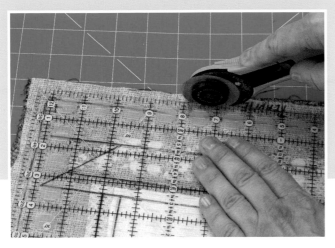

Opportunity Number 1

If your blocks end up being a bit larger than the pattern calls for, you can trim them all to a larger size and then adjust the lattice and any other affected pieces. Be aware, however, that the traced outside line may show through very light fabric.

Opportunity Number 2

If your blocks end up a bit smaller than the pattern indicates, you can add a strip to the side or two that are lacking.

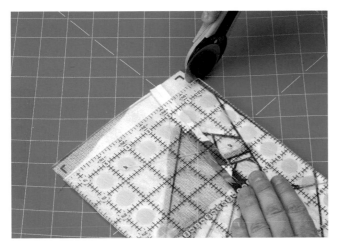

Opportunity Number 3

If some blocks are smaller than the pattern size, you can opt to trim all the blocks down to the smaller size. If lattice and borders are precut, just trim them to adjust to the new measurements. This is a creative choice that you are certainly welcome to make. If you feel the block is actually more pleasing in a smaller size, I won't mind! Thank you for sparing my feelings by letting it happen via a creative opportunity, but you really can just say you want the block smaller!

Precision Trimming

Perhaps you have taken the creative leap to use the "wrong" side of the fabric, and after piecing it, you just aren't happy with the results. There is still no reason to pull out the seam ripper. While I wouldn't object to you loosening the stitches and sliding them out of the fabric, I don't think it's necessary. You may need to get rid of that fabric in your block, but there is a way to eliminate it without removing stitches. Yes, everything is an opportunity waiting to happen!

Opportunity Number 1

There is another skill that we haven't honed in this book yet: precision trimming. This is such a valuable skill for removing fabric, and I'm delighted to share it with you.

Grab the seam allowances on the piece you are removing. Trim as close to the stitching line as possible without disturbing the stitches. On the other side of the seam line, do the same with the patch of fabric.

Now comes the really fun part! Do you see the little row of fibers caught in the stitching line? You now get to pick at those little strands and free them from the stitching line. How fun is that! I just love this step! If that is a bit too much fun for you to handle, you could certainly leave the ridge of fibers in and cover them when you add the new piece. Bonus texture!

Making Continuous Bias Binding

Some quilters avoid bias binding like the plague, but I rather like that it can become an interesting design element on my quilts. While there are different techniques to make bias binding, I go for the simplest, fastest way! For example, in step 3, many people would mark where the cuts should go, but I just go ahead and whack a leader cut. I like to have rolls of binding ready, so I make continuous bias out of big honkin' squares and set it aside to use on later quilts. It's terrific to finish quilting and know that the bias binding is ready to roll! (Sorry, I couldn't resist.)

1 Start with a 36" square of fabric. Make sure the lengthwise grain runs evenly across top, and corners are true 90°. Fold the square in half (right-sides together), opposite corners together, creating a triangle. Line up the triangle point and the center of the fold, cut. Producing two triangles.

2 With right sides together, match up the two straight-grain edges to make a pair of triangle pants. Sew that seam from edge to edge. (This produces a parallelogram for all you geometry buffs.) Press seam open.

3 Lay one of the points flat on a cutting board and make a leader cut the width of your binding and approximately 3 inches long. I use 2¼" binding.

4 Grab the new point created by cutting the leader, and line that straight-grain edge up with the opposite straight-grain edge, right sides together. Let the new point stick past the opposite corner to start the ¼" seam. The leader strip will be hanging loose. Once the seam is sewn, it becomes a tube.

5 Sew seam together and press open.

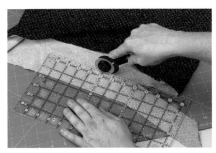

6 Starting at the leader strip, cut the continuous strip in your desired binding width. Just keep cutting and cutting, the end is near!

7 With wrong sides together, fold the strip in half lengthwise and press. My grandmother taught me to roll it around an empty spool or cardboard cereal box. This keeps it pressed and ready to attach at a moment's notice.

Conclusion

In one of the first quilting classes I took at a local shop, I was so excited to be there making a quilt! As we were sewing, the instructor was walking around the classroom checking out our work. When she got to me, she looked down and said, "Well, I suppose if *you* can live with that." After the shock and hurt wore off, I decided I could live with that. Quilting is not only about the end result, it is about the process. The journey is filled with joy, and I encourage you to not let criticism or stress interfere with the celebration. I hope you don't leave any quilting experience discouraged or lacking confidence—just see it as a door to new opportunities.

Resources

FABRIC:

Avlyn Fabrics
1628 West Williams Drive
Phoenix, AZ 85027
866-564-5426
E-mail: info@avlyn.com

Bali Fabrics
21787 Eighth St. East Suite #1
Sonoma, CA 95476
800-783-4612
E-mail: batik@balifab.com
www.balifab.com

E.E. Schenck Co.
6000 N. Cutter Circle
Portland, OR 97217
800-433-0722
Fax: 800-433-0723

Island Batik, Inc.
2719 Loker Ave. West, Suite B
Carlsbad, CA 92008
Voice: 760-602-0607
Toll Free: 888-522-2845
Fax: 760-602-0609
E-mail: islandbatik@sbc-global.net
www.islandbatik.com

Marcus Fabrics
Marcus Brothers Textiles, Inc.
980 Avenue of the Americas
New York, NY 10018
212-354-8700
Fax: 212-354-5245
www.marcusfabrics.com

Red Rooster Fabrics
1349 Broadway Suite 1202
New York NY 10018
212-244-6596
Fax: 212-760-1536
www.redroosterfabrics.com

Robert Kaufman Fabrics
Box 59266 Greenmead Station
Los Angeles, CA 90059-0266
800-877-2066
E-mail: info@robertkaufman.com

**Joel Dewberry for
Westminster Fibers, Inc.**
Fabrics Division
3430 Toringdon Way, Suite 301
Charlotte, NC 28277
E-mail: sarah.bailey@westminsterfibers.com
www.westminsterfabrics.com

SUPPLIES:

Specialty Product Sales, Inc.
15155 Bailey Hill Road
Brooksville, FL 34614
352-797-9019

Add-A-Quarter™

CM Designs, inc.
7968 Kelty Trail
Franktown, CO 80116
303-841-5920
www.addaquarter.com

**No-Show
Mesh Stabilizer**

Baby Lock
Tacony Manufacturing
#3 Industrial Dr.
St. James, MO 65559
573-265-0500
Fax: 537-265-0600
www.babylock.com

Sulky of America
980 Cobb Place Blvd., Suite 130
Kennesaw, GA 30144
800-874-4115

About the Author

What can I tell you about myself that you don't already know? You know I have four kids, a hubby and a dog. I live in Minnesota and my studio is in my basement. That is the basic stuff. Let's see—did you know that I have degrees in theatre and voice performance? I graduated with papers that say I sing and act. My dad thought perhaps I should have something more substantial or useful, like a teaching degree. I disagreed then, and I disagree now.

I have never had a desire to teach in a general classroom setting. Discipline is not something I'm good at or look forward to using. I do direct the sixth-grade musical at my children's school each year, but I get to sweep in and sweep out. I get the very best of them.

Before I had children, I taught beginning piano students and voice students. That kind of teaching I love! I especially enjoy adult students that missed the childhood piano lessons and are hungry to learn. They are not unlike my quilting students now. We come together to the classroom to learn, play, and be together. Whether it is a piano or voice lesson, a lecture or a hands-on class, the opportunity to connect is there. Not willing to completely sever my music ties, I always keep at least one voice student along with directing the musical. The students have ranged from serious vocalists to athletes who just love to sing! Whatever the ultimate goal, the function of the lesson is musical joy.

Shared joy makes it very difficult to keep detached. I have long had the reputation of being more than just the voice teacher. My students become part of my family and are forever in our lives. I adore them and the time that we have spent together building skills and a relationship.

Building skills and a relationship is just what I do as a quilting teacher. Whether the relationship is between teacher and student, between fellow students, or between a student and the fabric, the magic happens. This book is here because of that magic. I love to share tidbits I've learned on my quilting journey, but what I've been able to impart is nothing compared to what I've gleaned from all of the fabulous students I've encountered.

See, Dad! I'm teaching!

Oh, by the way, I've written a slew of patterns and couple of other books before this one. Check them out on my Website (www. crosscutsquilting.com) if you get a minute. Better yet, drop me a note from the site. I'd love nothing more than to hear what you've been working on. Life is full of opportunities; let's connect.

Index

More fun fast fabulous quilting!

No-Stress Foundation Piecing

13 Projects
Using Flannel or Cotton

Carolyn Cullinan McCormick

Gain insider instruction for using easy-to-follow techniques and the essential Add-A-Quarter™ tools to incorporate flannel and cotton fabrics into your paper piecing quilt projects. Contains a CD with 13 projects, including lap and baby quilts.

Paperback

8½" × 11"

175 color photos 100 b& w illustrations

Item # Z0764

ISBN-10: 0-89689-493-2

ISBN-13: 978-0-89689-493-8

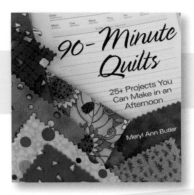

90-Minute Quilts

25+ Projects
You Can Make in an Afternoon

Meryl Ann Butler

Discover how easy it is to create stylish baby and large lap quilts, plus wall hangings using the quick, tips and methods 250 how-to color photos and illustrations included in this book.

Hardcover

8" × 8"

250 color photos and illustrations

Item # NTYMQ

ISBN-10: 0-89689-325-1

ISBN-13: 978-0-8968-932-5

Barbara Randle's More Crazy Quilting With Attitude

Barbara Randle

Three trendy techniques enable quilters and sewers to create 14 crazy-quilting projects including a throw, diaper bag, a variety of handbags and a gallery of customized clothing. Ideal for all skill levels with full-size patterns included.

Paperback

8¼" ×10⅞"

160 color photos and illustrations

Item # CQWA2

ISBN-10: 0-87349-975-1

ISBN-13: 978-0-87349-975-0

These and other fine Krause Publications books are available at your local craft retailer, bookstore or online supplier. Or visit our Website at
www.mycraftivity.com.